£2

PARKSIDE COLLIERY

The Birth, Life and Death of the last pit
in the old Lancashire Coalfield

First published 1994 by
Geoff Simm, 19 Park Road North,
Newton-le-Willows WA12 9TF
Tel: (01925) 224088.

ISBN 0 9524787 0 6

Design by Geoff Simm

Printed by Willow Printing 75/79 Back Cross Lane,
Newton-le-Willows, Merseyside WA12 9YE
Tel: (01925) 222449 or 228524.

Acknowledgements

I gratefully acknowledge the help given by the following people: Sid Hichisson, for collecting a large amount of information about Parkside and its personnel, Cliff Daniels, Ron Silver, Peter Dooley, Norman Harrison, Eric Speight, George Shaw, Wally Thomas, Graham Carr, Ian Winstanley, Frank Reid, Alan Sinar, John Watkins, Bert Dyer, Jeff Booth, Stan Horsfield, Frank King, Ray Bolton, Eric Dear, Roy Lythgoe, Boris Nabakow, Adam Kuzio, Billy Ablitt, Frank Grimshaw and Kate Atkinson.

I would like also to take this opportunity to thank three people for putting up with me over the years. I started work with Jack Woodcock, Roy Fairhurst and John Horrocks as an apprentice over thirty years ago and was still working with them at the end of the pit's life.

Part One

The History of the Colliery

Parkside Colliery nearing completion.

PRELIMINARIES

During the late 1940's and the early 1950's the newly formed National Coal Board embarked on a major boring operation throughout the southern part of the South Lancashire Coal-field. The intention was to confirm the sequence of known coal seams southward towards the Cheshire plain. The results of that programme caused the Board to re-develop and expand some of the more important collieries in the district; Sutton Manor, Clock Face, Bold, Astley Green, Mosely Common and Agecroft were all re-developed in some form or other to gain access to those reserves. Some of the changes were limited to underground restructuring, but others led to the complete rebuilding of the colliery. However, south of Haydock, it was decided to open a completely new colliery. It was thought that the two pits in that area, Wood Pit and Lyme Pits, did not justify large investments. Great excitement must have been felt at all levels of the local Coal Board hierarchy at that time. A new colliery was to be built in Lancashire, the first for 35 years, with enough coal for over 100 years of mining!

The boring programme began as early as 1947, when the first borehole was drilled at Park Road, Newton-le-Willows. Further boring, started in 1950, south of Newton, established reserves of over 115 million tons of coal in the proposed extraction area.

In 1952, a group of German scientists were invited to check the results of the borings using new methods of surveying strata. The results of that scientific study were so encouraging that it was decided that a new colliery should be sunk in the area.

The initial planning of the new colliery was begun as early as April 1953. Later that year a meeting discussing the preliminary aims was convened at Bold Colliery. Present at the meeting were all the major figures in the No.3 (St.Helens) Area of the National Coal Board:-

Mr.F.G.Glossop - Divisional Production Director
Mr.J.Anderton - Area General Manager
Mr.L.C.Timms - Area Production Manager
Mr.F.Sinar - Divisional Planning Engineer
Mr.F.B.Armstrong - Area Planning Engineer
Mr.M.P.Coleman - Area Chief Planning Surveyor

More meetings were held later in 1953, they checked all reports from the surveys and discussed the required water supply, shaft positions and production levels. By November 1953 the name of the new colliery had been decided on - Parkside.

In April 1954, the NCB chief planning engineer, Mr.F.Marsh, visited the Area Office and talked over the project with J.Anderton, L.C.Timms,

F.B.Armstrong, F.Sinar, E.W.Dear and A.Johnson. The points raised included Horizon mining, available reserves and the site of the colliery. Eric Dear, who later became the area planning engineer, attended some of the meetings in the early days:-

"There was a feeling of great enthusiasm about the Parkside project during the meetings. Every technical innovation was examined to see whether it would fit our overall plan for the colliery; some of them were successful others were not."

During June 1954 a planning office was set up at Mere House, Newton-le-Willows, where Alf Johnson and Roy Lythgoe began the detailed plan of Parkside Colliery. By that time the position of the colliery was limited to 4 sites (see map below). James Anderton and his team of experts finally decided on site 'C' for the colliery. The favourable points were the shallower depth of seams, absence of water bearing strata near the shafts, easier access to the main highway and easier access to the railway.

The name of the colliery probably came from the position of Site 'A', which was at Parkside farm, just off Parkside Road. It was originally to be called Newton Colliery, but there were objections from the local authority, who did not want a colliery named after them and it was also pointed out that there had already been a Newton Colliery previously in the district.

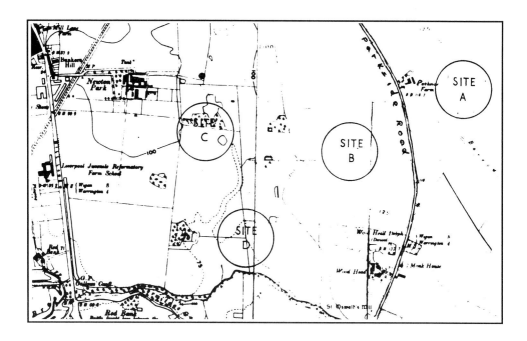

The Press finally got wind of the project in January 1955 when a report appeared in the Evening Chronicle about the NCB buying land to sink a new colliery. Also, later in the year, Fred Lee, the MP for Newton, asked for a statement from the Minister of Agriculture about valuable agricultural land being used for coal production.

In March 1955 Newton Park Farm was purchased from Mr. Bridge, the owner/occupier, for the sum of £28,000. There is evidence that it was done in some secrecy, with an intermediary being used. Alan Sinar, the son of Frank Sinar, recalls his father saying that the site was purchased under the name of an accountant, hiding the fact that the NCB was involved.

By 1955, Alf Johnson was well established as the Parkside planner. He and Roy Lythgoe liaised with Dr. Jan Bakker and P.T.H.Velzeboer, the chief NCB experts on Horizon mining, and made many visits to London for detailed consultations.

Due to the amount of information which had to be analysed, meetings were held more frequently. The positions of local boreholes were being studied to give more information on the strata close to the proposed shafts. Also, the Area Electricity Board visited the site to assess the provision of a temporary supply. Yet no application for planning permission had been officially made to any of the local authorities. That application was finally made to the Newton, Golborne and Warrington Urban District Councils on May 9th, 1955.

Drilling of local boreholes.

Parkside was officially announced to the country on July 13th, 1955, when a luncheon was held for Press, NCB and local dignitaries. The day after, the news appeared in local and national papers and was mentioned in a BBC 8am news bulletin. The report in the Newton & Earlestown Guardian read as follows:-

"A new mine which is to be sunk at Parkside, Newton, is to cost £10,000,000, employ 2,200 men and produce, when in full production, 1,000,000 tons of good quality coal in a year. The

sinking of the new mine to be called Parkside, was announced at a press conference at the Divisional Coal Board in Manchester on Wednesday."

At the colliery site the local boreholes were drilled in August 1955 and on the 16th of that month the unions were informed about the new project.

A long delay now ensued before town and country planning permission was granted. No decision was made at the Inquiry held on 29th May 1956, with it being referred to the Ministry of Housing and Local Government. The decision to allow the NCB to sink Parkside Colliery was granted by October 1956, with certain restrictive recommendations, relating to the protection of local buildings, waterways, roads and sewers. The official permission was granted as follows:-

For the sinking of shafts, the erection of buildings and the carrying out of other development required in connection with colliery production activities (except the disposal of waste material) within the areas shown hatched vertically on the annexed plan, subject to the following conditions:-

(1) Details of the design and lay-out of the buildings shall be as may be agreed with the local planning authority or, in default of agreement by the Minister.

(2) Measures for the landscape treatment of the site shall be carried out in accordance with such scheme, which may include provision for the planting of trees and shrubs and the disposal of soil and other materials, as may be agreed with the local planning authority or, in default of agreement, as shall be determined by the Minister.

(3) The construction of the proposed access to the A49 trunk road shall be carried out as may be agreed with the local planning authority in consultation with the highway authority or, in default of agreement, as shall be determined by the Minister.

For the winning and working of coal in any seam found under the area shown outlined by a bold black line on the annexed plan, subject to the following conditions:-

(1) A pillar of support shall be left under the County Mental Hospital at Winwick and the extent of this pillar shall be as may be agreed with the local planning authority or, in default of agreement, as shall be determined by the Minister.

(2) Such coal shall be left unworked for the support of the Sankey Valley sewer and for the protection of the existing built-up area within the present boundary of the County Borough of Warrington as may be agreed with the local planning authority or, in default of agreement, as shall be determined by the Minister.

The above planning permission gave the green light for the Parkside Colliery project. Arrangements were made with the surface contractors towards the end of the year, regarding a starting date. All preparations were complete, everybody was ready to begin their great task in the new year -- the construction of Parkside Colliery.

BEGINNINGS.

The proposed colliery site was entered on the 1st February 1957. Throughout the first month preliminary work was done on the stripping of the top soil, laying of a temporary road and commencement of work on the drainage system. Roy Lythgoe, who later became the colliery surveyor and had worked with Alf Johnson for many months on the Parkside project, recalls starting work in the fields:-

"We started work in the fields of Newton Park Farm, setting up the base lines and pegging out the site. When the top soil was cleared off, the Winwick fault could be clearly seen in the sandstone. It ran from north to south through the future position of the manager's office."

Surveyors in the fields of Newton Park Farm.

Within a few months the permanent access road had been laid by Fairclough, together with the small bridge over the farm track and the weigh bridge. It was felt that the surface buildings should be constructed in accordance with an overall plan, and temporary buildings kept to a minimum. The development of the main surface buildings was carried out in four distinct phases. Phase one was the construction of the main office block, it being used for the temporary offices, baths, workshops, stores, canteen and substation. Phase two was the construction of the boiler house and baths. Phase three was the main baths canteen and pay hall. The last phase was to convert the phase one buildings to their permanent use.

Parkside Colliery foundation stone was laid on the 28th May 1957, to great acclaim in the local Press. The stone was laid by Mrs Bolton, the wife of Colonel Bolton, Chairman of the North Western Divisional Board. Present at the ceremony were local, NCB and council dignitaries. James Anderton, Area General Manager, made the official speech:-

"Although many people think coal mines are now old fashioned and of little use, with atomic power just around the corner, coal is still of vital importance to the nation, and with the advances in those powers it will play an even bigger part, thus calling for an increasing yield from coal-fields. The country needs coal now more than ever before, and by 1970 the NCB are aiming to produce 250 million tons of coal each year. To-day, we are launching one of the units to achieve that object and so improve our standard of living. Parkside Colliery will be the first colliery to be built in Lancashire for 35yrs. Many of our collieries have reached their centenary and some are even many years older. If we are to maintain production in Lancashire, we must replace these old collieries with new ones because old collieries are like old soldiers - they fade away."

Stone Laying Ceremony
Left: James Anderton. Right: Mrs Bolton.

Afterwards, there was a buffet laid on in a large open marquee and music was provided during the proceedings by the Clock Face & Sutton Manor Colliery Bands. Colonel Bolton closed the proceedings with a short speech thanking everybody for their work so far on the project.

Such a large industrial and building project, that Parkside became, required large amounts of manual labour. Men came from all parts of the country; mostly Irish labour attracted by the heavy work and good wages. They were hard men doing hard work which went some way to stimulating the local economy. Some of them would relax for many hours in the local pubs, being relieved of their hard earned money by the female camp followers that had become attracted to the area. At night men could be found sleeping in the farm barns and in the concrete drainage pipes that were stacked on the site. A supply industry was set up by the local Co-op van, which provided most of the food to the workmen. One man craftily took control of the ordering and it is said that he retired to Ireland, buying his own farm with the proceeds from the "Divi". On the whole it was a time of hard, dirty and wet work, typical of any large construction job, requiring a certain type of worker to carry it out.

Throughout the Summer of 1957 work was carried out on the construction of the Phase one surface buildings. The first building to be completed was the Magazine, quickly followed by the main office block and baths. However, the majority of the work was the preparation for the priority job - the sinking of the shafts.

SINKING.

By June 1957 the contract for the sinking of the shafts had been given to Kinear - Moodie, a British construction company. They employed a South African company, Roberts Construction, to oversee the sinking of the shafts. Roberts Construction provided gang bosses and a team of 12 men led by Mr. C. McLauchlan, who acted as technical adviser. The reason why South Africans were used at Parkside was that during the war years they had been developing high speed sinking methods in their own country. The fact that there had been little shaft sinking in Britain for many years meant that there was little expertise in that field.

Work was begun almost immediately on what was termed the fore-shafts. The pre-sinking work was carried out using a steam crane fitted with a cactus grab. At that early stage temporary arrangements were used for dirt clearance and shaft concreting using a temporary staging. Only weeks into the initial sinking operation tragedy struck in No.1 shaft when 2 men, William Green and Thomas Walsh, were killed on the night shift. During concreting operations the hoppit ran into the staging and dislodged it, sending the two men to their deaths.

Shaft sinking operations - summer 1957.

To speed up operations the two sinking headgears were constructed away from the shafts and towed across when completed. The No.2 Headgear was moved into position on August 31st and on October 4th the No.1 Headgear was positioned over its shaft. No.1 headgear was designed at Haydock Foundry and constructed by Naylors of Golborne, the locally renowned engineering firm.

The fore-shafts were sunk to a depth of approximately 50yds, to enable the construction and fitting of the 3 deck sinking scaffolds or platforms. The sinking teams then took over and commenced their work on the shafts; No.1 being started on November 24th, 1957 and No.2 on the December 1st.

The two shafts were sunk simultaneously over the next two years by two separate teams combining South African and multi-national workers. The policy was to keep men of the same nationality together to assist communication during the work.

Tragedy again struck the new colliery on December 4th, when there was an accident in No.2 Shaft. A man called E.Kuraj, was killed and 2 men were injured. The ascending hoppit caught on the scaffold and tipped over, burying the three men.

Because the two shafts were being sunk simultaneously, both shaft teams vied with each other to see who was the fastest. George Shaw, the No.1 shaft winder, remembers working at the pit:-

"There was great competition between us and Danny Jones, the winder at No.2 shaft. But we had one thing in our favour, our grab driver on the platform was very fast, so we always had the edge."

The sinking platforms that were used at Parkside Colliery were designed and constructed at Haydock Central Works. Cyril Lambert recalls his work on the project:-

"I was draughtsman on the No.1 Headgear and the sinking platform. The basic design came from the mechanical department and we ironed out the problems and produced the drawings."

Len Worthington remembers working on the construction of the platform at Haydock:-

"The 3-deck platform was built in the Boiler shop at Haydock Foundry. The man in charge of its construction was Bill Belshaw who was really proud of his connection with the sinking of Parkside."

Early visits to the colliery
Above: NCB Top Brass.
Below: Tom Hulme, Billy Ablitt, Fred Lee MP & Mr Glossop inside the hoppit.

During the initial sinking operations the manager of Parkside Colliery was George Herbert Harrison. Previously he had been manager at Sutton Manor and Clock Face Collieries and had been brought out of semi-retirement to oversee the work at Parkside. When he worked at Parkside he was known as a friendly and likable man who sadly suffered from ill health. Possibly he was not the man for such a demanding job, with all its problems and the eyes of the Coal Board hierarchy upon him. Various other semi-retired managers were used at Parkside until the establishment of Albert Taylor, a group manager in the St.Helens Area. Albert Taylor was a tough, domineering and commanding figure, ideally suited to deal with the situation and the South African management, who tended to ride rough-shod over rules and regulations. Peter Dooley, the later deputy manager, remembers him well:-

"Albert Taylor was a straight talking individual with great ability and was much respected by his peers."

A.E.Taylor was Group Manager of Bold, Sutton Manor and Clock Face Collieries and was probably hoping to spend the rest of his working days in that job. However, due to the respect that James Anderton had for him, he was persuaded, with some reluctance, to take on the Parkside project.

The three deck sinking platform used in the sinking of the pit was 40 tons in weight and contained the majority of the equipment required for the sinking operations; slings and jacks to secure the platform, winches and the main grab that was used for mucking out and special shuttering for the concreting. Successful operation of such a platform required skill, detailed planning, strength and stamina from the men. The work was wet, dirty and difficult, carried out on three shifts with no rest in between. Tony Curtis, the No.2 pit banksman can remember the men coming up the pit:-

"The men in the shaft worked in the worse conditions that I've ever seen. After mucking out they would come up the pit covered in sweat and also wet through. They would throw their clothes over the pipes in the drying room, have a drink and then back down the pit."

Tony's real name was Bartholomew, but all his working life at Parkside he was known as Tony, after the film star. He later worked in the skip discharge and then became 1A Winder. Tony was a very careful engineman, only running the engines at half speed. When asked for the reason, he would reply that the sooner he got there the sooner he would be coming back!

Concrete was delivered from the surface to the platform via a 6 inch pipe, which was extended as the shaft deepened. Two small conveyors ran to the shafts from the mixing station situated mid-way between the two

Above: Sinking headgears fully operational.
Below: Bottom of one of the shafts after clearing operations.

shafts. The men who controlled the mixing station were on call 24 hrs a day, having to report immediately when required. Billy Ablitt was the No.1 Pit Banksman at that time:-

"The noise was terrific when concreting started and the further we got down the more violent it became. Sparks as long as 3 ft would shoot out of the pipe joints as the concrete rushed past."

During the initial shaft sinking blasting was done by normal battery, but then mains firing was used after a special approval was granted in March 1958. Eric Speight was the electrical engineer throughout the early years of the colliery and remembers why mains firing was used:-

"The sinkers requested mains parallel firing because of the problems they had encountered with series firing in wet conditions and high salt deposits. The inspectorate insisted on specialised making up of rounds on the surface and strict control was kept on the sinkers' methods. It was a continual battle between the NCB staff, who were trying to stay within the regulations, and the South African sinkers, who were only thinking of their daily sinking rate."

The South Africans had early problems with the blasting operations due to the type of strata they encountered. They were used to sinking through hard rock and at first couldn't cope with the loose shales they met with at Parkside. George Shaw recalls one of the problems:-

"They were using too much powder during the firing. It was only when Peter Lamb, the NCB shot-firer, took over that things improved. Some of the holes that the South Africans were blowing, you could fit Liverpool Cathedral in."

One other trick the shaft teams were guilty of was leaving any extra powder underground, to go off with rest. Billy Ablitt had a close call during one of his relaxing moments:-

"The swines left a pile of powder down with a Det. stuck in it. The blast blew all the flooring out of the platform, spun the hoppit round at ground level, blew the corrugated sheets off the headgear and knocked me out of the cabin. I was stuck for words for half an hour."

To people who knew Billy Ablitt, the last remark would have been most unusual!

After the initial teething problems the sinking operations greatly increased in speed. No.1 Shaft was forced to stop at 600 ft because of the amount of water encountered. The shaft team had to seal all the water

Above:
Albert Taylor & Sister Fish.

Right: Wally Thomas.

feeders before sinking could re-commence. At first a target of 185 ft per month was attained, then an average of 250 ft was reached and maintained. Finally a record of 309 ft was attained in No.1 shaft during the month of September 1958. This was a record for a completely furnished shaft, that is to say, concreted and all pipes and fittings installed. Parkside was to set the precedence for all future shaft sinkings, regarding planning and application. Roy Lythgoe, the colliery surveyor, devised a method to keep the shafts vertically on line. He later produced a paper on the subject and it was used in other parts of the world. The photographs of the shaft sinking teams shows the smiling faces of men proud of their achievement in the face of terrible working conditions. Wally Thomas. one of the first NCB men employed at the pit, remembers starting at Parkside:-

"There were six deputies employed by the Coal Board when I started in 1958: Me, Harold Craggs, Tommy Fyldes, Jack Mawdsley, Harry Mayer and Sammy Johnson. We covered the three shifts, one man in either shaft, with no days off. The only problem we had was that we were the only men working in the shafts not on bonus."

Wally Thomas later became the official over some of the drivages and during the production days was the afternoon overman. His memories about the sinking of Parkside are still very clear:-

"Not a minute was wasted in the shaft during all three cycles. After firing, the sinking team would go down so quickly that we would meet the smoke coming up. It was wet, hard and dirty work carried out with the utmost speed. The overall South African boss was McLauchlan, but the shaft bosses were MacAlpine and Scott, who were both giants. They tended to ride rough shod over everybody, but the man that kept them under control was Albert Taylor, the manager, who was feared and respected by every man at the pit."

The sinking of Parkside shafts was carried out by a truly cosmopolitan workforce; Italians, Irish, Germans, Poles and South Africans were all represented. Some of them slept rough on site but the majority were lodged locally. In 1958, a local colliery nurse, Sister Fish, was invited to visit the pit on a half-day a week basis. She can still remember attempting to look after the welfare of the sinkers:-

"The sinkers were, on the whole, a decent gang of lads. Some of them would ask me to look after their wages overnight, until they could get to the bank to send it home. I sometimes had a thousand pounds in my

Shaft sinking teams.
Above: No.1 Shaft. Below: No. 2 Shaft.

hands. A mobile shop came from Burtonwood Air Base on Thursdays, after the men had been paid. It sold American whiskey, cigarettes and cigars. I've seen hundreds of pounds change hands in a matter of minutes."

There were many temptations for the workers at the pit; drink and loose women were just two of them. At one time some local prostitutes had established themselves behind the colliery Magazine. Sister Fish can well remember chasing them off with the aid of Bill Evans, the pit bobby.

Sister Fish later became the permanent nurse at the colliery and looked on Parkside as an important part of her life. Having no children of her own, its men became her family and she looked after their health and welfare with great zeal, even though some of the management wanted just a plaster sticker.

The shaft sinking at Parkside took nearly two years, both shafts being completed within a few weeks of each other; No.1 on February 13th and No.2 on March 3rd, 1959.

TOWERS.

It was just before the completion of the shaft sinking that work began on the raising of Parkside towers. A decision was made to maintain continuity by offering the contract to Roberts Construction, the South African partners of Kinear - Moodie. The company was conversant in their own country with the method of construction that was used at Parkside. A Mr. Alec Combrink was invited over to take charge at the colliery during the tower construction. His thoughts on the subject have survived in the form of a paper he produced after the work was completed:-

"The Parkside story for my part could be said to have begun at the beginning of July 1958, when I was asked by Mr. Roberts whether I would come over to the United Kingdom to manage this Contract. The next three weeks were one long rush in preparing to come over and it was really not until I got here that I knew very much about Parkside."

Work commenced on No.1 tower in October 1958, when excavations began for the tower foundations. After the foundations were completed the first 29 ft were built using conventional shuttering methods. This decision was made because the shaft sinking was still being carried out. When the tower was completed to the 29 ft level the sliding shuttering platform was assembled and fitted. For concreting purposes a scaffolding tower was erected alongside the tower. Alec Combrink's paper gives information on the construction:-

"By its very nature of working around the clock sliding shuttering construction requires a very large number of men for a comparatively short time. In this particular case we were very fortunate in being able to get the

requisite number of men without a very long build-up, and whilst they were obviously initially some what at sea, they very quickly caught on to what was required and within a few days of starting developed into a very good team. This was, of course, most gratifying. The supervisory aspect, of course, also proved a considerable problem and an engineer experienced in this form of construction was flown out from South Africa to assist me and supervise the night shift.

The slide was commenced on the 27th February and completed on the 19th March, a total of 20 days, during which time we had a stoppage of three days at deflector floor level, to connect up with shutters supported here on a second scaffold tower. It was at this time we had our only labour troubles, when our steel fixing contractor went bankrupt. From here onwards we took on our own steel-fixers and our troubles in this connection were over. In spite of its increased height of slide - in all 30ft - No. 2 Tower was slid in only 18 days, which indicates the value of even a little experience by the men in this sort of work. During the slide we placed something like 2,500 cu. yds. of concrete and fixed approximately 180 tons of steel. Approximately 60 men were employed on each shift: that is labourers, steel fixers and joiners."

Night view of tower construction.

"Many of you might have seen the job by night, and you will therefore appreciate the considerable amount of work which was put into the wiring up of the pumps, etc., and, of course, all the lights. The working deck and sliding shutters were supported on 70 jacks, which in turn climbed up 1in diameter mild steel bars which remained behind in the

*Above and right:
Construction of winding
towers.*

concrete. The jacks are actuated by two hydraulic pumps which develop a pressure of 2-3000 psi. The net stroke of the jacks is 3/4in. but the rate of jacking has to be varied to suit the rate of fixing of boxes for reinforcing steel and, of course, concrete, and the rate varied between 6 minutes per cycle and 20 minutes in the more difficult places. The depth of the shutter was 4 ft and therefore at the maximum rate of jacking, concrete was being exposed with seven hours of placing. A hanging scaffold was provided below the shutters and from this scaffold 'rubbers up' wood-floated the concrete to remove any unsightly streaks."

The main body of the tower, from the ground level to the deflector floor, is of box construction with walls 20in. thick. The section above, comprising deflector, intermediate and winder floors, is reduced down to 8in. thick. These three floors and their equipment are supported by two 10 ft thick post stressed beams situated under the deflector floor. The two beams between them have 32 cables, each cable consisting of twenty four 7mm. high tensile wires, stressed to a load of 95 tons.

When the towers reached their full height a special 'topping out' ceremony was carried out, with drinks to celebrate their achievement.

The complicated process described above produced the most distinctive aspect of Parkside colliery - its Towers. They have been referred to in many different ways: 'industrial architecture', 'those horrible grey monsters' and 'bloody eyesores'.

Parkside towers, throughout their life, were used for many things, some of them lawful and some not: surveying, circuit training, sun bathing, astronomy, radio ham transmission and, last of all, a pit protest by the Women against Pit Closures.

The most remarkable tale is of the 'flying cat'. A number of years ago, one of the pit cats was launched from No.1 tower connected to a previously tested parachute. All worked well, with the cat floating safely to earth. At 50ft up, the cat began running and when it landed it vanished into the next field, never to be seen again!

FITTING OUT

In the summer of 1959, after the completion of the sinking operations, work began on the construction of the insets. No.1 Horizon had already been done during the sinking, but the others were constructed in ascending order. A deck was fitted below the position of the inset and sealed with wooden baulks, a concrete layer and any loose debris. Checks were made periodically to ensure there was no build up of gas below the decks. The work on the insets was to take up the majority of that year, with it being completed by December 1959.

Cutting out of insets.

After the insets were constructed and the shafts cleared, it was found that they had filled with water to a depth of 400ft. To drain this water two of the sinking hoppits were converted to wind water, it taking three weeks to empty the shafts. Next, connections were made between the two shafts and work began on the fitting out of No.1 shaft. It was necessary that the fitting out of No.1 shaft was done quickly, to enable work to begin on the Horizon tunnels. Information on the fitting out of No.1 shaft was put down in a paper given by Alf Johnson and William Holdsworth in 1962:-

"When the shaft had been completed and handed over by the sinking contractor, a single deck scaffold of NCB manufacture was installed. The sinking services were next removed and the work of shaft equipping commenced. To facilitate the equipping of the buntons, pipes and cables, the scaffold was designed to work in conjunction with two equipping cages, which had been specially built for this work. Each cage held one bunton and a complete set of pipes to take it down to the next bunton approximately 75 ft below. The cage was also fitted with a derrick and winch and when positioned in the shaft the pipes were lowered from the cage to the scaffold by means of the derrick, the second cage meanwhile was being loaded at the surface. When the buntons and pipes had been completed a super-structure was fitted to the equipping scaffold and cable drums were mounted on the platform, as the platform was lowered the cable was payed off the drum and cleated to the buntons by men positioned on the super-structure. With this system it was possible to install two cables simultaneously, which proved a safe and efficient system and certainly saved some time over the normal rope method of installation.

On completion of this section of the work the installation of inset steel work was commenced at each horizon in turn. The inset decking equipment is of Westinghouse manufacture and consists of platforms with outer arms."

Eric Speight was in charge of the installation of the electrical equipment in the shafts:-

"The furnishing of the shafts was a top priority job, with the power, interlock and signal cables being installed two at a time. At the surface and insets, Westinghouse equipment was used on the platforms and ram gear. Also photo-electric cells were used to give the final indication of position to the winder. They were later discontinued due to adverse conditions in the shaft causing problems."

Whilst the above work was being carried out, the connections between the two shafts at all three horizons were being driven from No.2 shaft, using the sinking winder and the existing hoppits for winding the dirt. A platform was fitted over the shaft at the level to be developed and the drivage commenced, using Eimco 622's loading into the hoppits mounted on bogies. The inset work, drivages from No.2 and the fitting out of No.1 shaft took two years to complete. The next major task at the colliery was the main tunnelling drivages in No.1, No.2 and No.3 Horizons, which began in April 1961.

Connecting tunnel between shafts.

DEVELOPMENT.

After the insets and the pit bottoms had been completed, work began on the driving of the main Horizon tunnels. When that work was complete there would be 9 miles of development tunnels at Parkside. On the NCB side, the person in charge of the majority of the development was Peter Dooley, who later became the deputy manager of the colliery:-

"My introduction to Parkside colliery was a rather a low key one. I was at that time undermanager at Wood Pit and was summoned to Parkside at very short notice. Having no transport, I was forced to get a lift in a coal lorry to the pit, where I waited for the arrival of the manager, Albert Taylor. He greeted me with the words, 'Where do you live', when I replied, 'St.Helens', he briefly commented, 'You'll have to flit'. That was my glorious entrance to Parkside colliery.

I moved to the colliery in January, 1961, the insets had been completed and my initial task was to oversee the driving of the main Horizon and development tunnels. The tunnelling contractor, George Wimpey & Co. took over early that year and commenced the cutting of the pit bottom circuits at No.1, 2 & 3 Horizons. Initially, extra precautions had to be taken, due to the danger of shot-firing so near to the shafts. The NCB manpower at that time was only 24 men underground. Wimpey's manpower, over the next few years, increased to a peak of 200 men. They were a rough and ready, gypsy type of worker, driven by money, but excellent tunnellers. At Parkside, they cut a series of tunnels that were a credit to the company, using basic machinery such as: Holman drills, various types of Eimco, shot-firing and just plain hard work. I well remember their bosses, who were characters in their own right: Richard Driver, Walter Pesh and probably best of all, Stan Draper. In No.1 and No.2 Horizons they had to drill up to 70 holes for a six foot take, but at No.3 up to 90 holes had to be done, due to the harder rock. As we approached the time for developing the first coal faces, their manpower reduced, with NCB men coming from the surrounding collieries that at that time were being closed."

Regarding the manpower, there were certain similarities with the shaft sinking, when nationalities were kept together. Boris Nabokow, a Wimpey chargehand, started work at the colliery after the tunnelling had commenced:-

"I started work on the No.2 and No.3 North tunnels in the early 1960's. I put together a team of men to cover three shifts, mostly Polish. men who knew each other and worked well together. We had a special price for extra yardage and on a good week could drive up to 45 metres of fully fitted tunnel. Speed was essential during tunnelling, not much talking, every man knew his job and carried it out quickly. If a man had nothing to

Above:
Completed horizon inset.

Right: Main fan drift.

do he helped the man next to him. We did very accurate drilling, so that there was no wastage to pack. The shot-firer had very little to do, we ran out and charged our own shots, knowing what type of detonator and the amount of explosive. The work was hard but we were paid good wages for that time, earning over £100 per week in 1963.

One job I do remember was in No.3 North. I was contracted to install a junction at the weekend for £2000. It took three of us, me, Stan Draper and Stan Wasylewski, two 18hr shifts to do the job, finishing at 4am Monday morning."

Boris Nabokow is typical of the men that came from the eastern block countries after the 2nd World War. Hard working, individualistic men, they were attracted to contract work in British coal mines because of the money. Boris originated from the Crimea, attended a Prussian Cadet school and then eventually was seconded into the British Army in the intelligence field. After the war he was employed by ATC, Wimpey, NCB and Cementation.

In April, 1961, a report appeared in the Colliery Guardian alluding to the colliery and its future:-

"Work has begun on the driving of 10 miles of tunnels to open up the coal faces at the new Parkside Colliery, Newton-le-Willows which will start production towards the end of next year. This phase in the construction of the £13 million colliery follows the completion of the underground connection between the two shafts, each nearly 900yds deep and 24ft in diameter. The tunnelling teams will drive outwards from the shafts, under south-west Lancashire, and make 40 junctions before their job is completed."

After the completion of the main development tunnels, it was decided to go for the top workable seam - the Crombouke. However, what had become apparent during the tunnelling, was a series of unforeseen faults in the coal measures. Roy Lythgoe reflects on the cause:-

"The local boreholes that were done throughout the site only proved the faulting in the overlying measures. It was assumed that any faulting there would appear in the carboniferous measures below. What was not realised that faulting had occurred in the coal bearing strata before the laying down of the upper measures. The deep boreholes that were done in the area only showed the positions of the major faults."

The problem with small irritating faults in the coal seams was to stay with the Parkside miners for many years to come. They only disappeared when coal production was concentrated south of the colliery, towards the Cheshire plain, away from the major faults in the north.

PRODUCTION.

Production officially began at Parkside Colliery in April, 1964. Dramatic headlines were splashed across the local papers heralding the 'Push Button Pit' and how it will soon produce a million tons a year. The newspaper quotes were typical of the time, full of correct and incorrect facts, written by people having little knowledge of mining. Below are a few examples:-

"The push button mining era came to Newton-le-Willows on Tuesday with the official opening of Parkside Colliery. The £13,000,000 showpiece of the NCB went into production with a 1,000 strong labour force - half the ultimate figure. The mine, which will eventually build up production to more than 1,000,000 tons a year, has a life expectancy of around 100 years."

"Underground, well-lit tunnels with flagged footpaths, lead to the various coal faces. And mantrains are soon to be installed to take the foot slogging out of mining."

"Mr. Harry Jackson of Park Street , Haydock, and Mr. John Smalley, of Westwood, Lower Ince, Wigan, both agreed Parkside was the finest pit they had ever worked in. Commented Mr. Jackson: 'Working conditions here are extremely comfortable'. And Mr. Smalley added: 'The back-breaking work has almost disappeared.'"

Albert Taylor, the agent-manager at that time commented to the local press:-

"This colliery compares with anything on the Continent and incorporates every new development and technique brought into the mining industry over the past few years."

The first coal face to be successfully developed and produce coal was B1, in No.2 South. Originally the first face was to be A1, in No.2 North, but during its development extensive faulting was discovered in the area, resulting in it being abandoned for some time. An attempt was made to open half of A1 face in 1967, but it only ran for 6 months.

Problems appeared immediately with the first faces, and the biggest of them all was water. B1 Face and its partner C1, which was cut off the same level, met with water within a matter of weeks. That part of the pit became known as the 'Water Caves', with some justification. The C1 Face, which was opened as a stopgap, due to the failure in developing A1, hardly accomplished anything and was abandoned by September, 1964. Besides the water problems on the face there was a small step in the middle that increased to 15ft after a month's production. Although there were great

Above: B1 Face.

Right: Visit of Roy Mason MP.
Left to right: Roy Green,
Roy Mason and Bill Holdsworth.

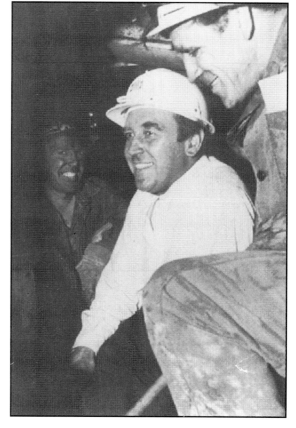

problems with conditions on B1 face it carried for some years. It was shortened back in 1965, creating what was termed at the pit 'the water brow' and then carried on until 1968, a life of 4 years. Peter Dooley, who was undermanager at that time, recollects the first major strike at the colliery:-

"The setting up and early production from B1 face went reasonably well, if sometimes erratic. C1 was opened up quickly to improve production, due to pressure being applied from area level for coal. However, as B1 advanced, water appeared and filtered to the lowest point in the area, which was C1 face. The conditions became intolerable for both men and management and coupled with a problem over piecework money it resulted in a short strike."

The strike over pay and conditions was eventually resolved but C1 face never reopened and the men were put on developments in other parts of the pit.

One of the shift electricians on C1 Face at that time was Brian Talbot, at the beginning of a career that was to take him near to the top of the Coal Board hierarchy. After attending a Ruskin College course Brian became interested in the Personnel and Industrial Relation fields. And, due to the many contacts he had encountered when captain of the first aid team, he quickly climbed a ladder of success. Brian Talbot, ex Parkside electrician and club bouncer, eventually became the Assistant Director of the Western Area, although he never lost his common touch.

There were also developments going on in the Crombouke seam in No.2 North, where the new F faces were being opened. The first of them, F1, was started in September 1964, but only ran till December of the same year. However, its neighbour, F6, which was started in May 1965, ran till 1968.

Throughout the early years the pit had terrible production troubles and failed to establish itself as a viable colliery. It became known as the 'White Elephant' and many of the old colliers laughed at the attempts to produce coal, commenting that Richard Evans & Co. would have sunk a pit there if it was profitable. By that time Albert Taylor had retired and his place was taken by his deputy, William Holdsworth, or 'Little Billy' as he was known to the men. He was a talkative and enthusiastic individual, of stocky build and great energy. He encouraged the men to take part in many pursuits besides coal mining, initiating the First Aid team, the Quiz team and through his enthusiasm he contributed to the pit winning the Area Safety Competition. The resulting prize money was used to fund the Parkside Gala of 1968, an enjoyable event that was repeated 12 months later.

From 1965 onwards, Bill Holdsworth, the Agent-Manager, and Peter Dooley, who had been promoted to Manager, had to wrestle with the great problems of the early faces. It was done with a workforce that was unused to

Above: **Parkside Lamproom.**
Left to right Ronnie Wilkins, Ernie Burgess and Alan Sinar.

Below: **Parkside Gala** *Jack Jaundrill and Maureen Broster.*

the pit and in some way unfamiliar with the new mining technology involved at the colliery.

In the 1960's, men working in the majority of the surrounding pits had little or no knowledge of the mechanisation that was required in a modern colliery. The pits in the locality, especially in the Wigan Area, were still using old fashioned methods of coal extraction, such as hand filled faces and primitive haulages. When the new workforce was transferred to Parkside some of them were overwhelmed with the scale of everything at the pit. Even the appearance of the towers and the first descent must have been daunting to some of the men. Sister Fish recalls:-

"They couldn't cope with the pit and the change in technology, even the height of the roadways caused psychological problems. It was such mental trauma that caused many of the men to leave, but some regretted the loss of their camaraderie and friendships."

Further development at the colliery was made in the Lower Florida Seam, one of the best quality coals available at Parkside. The first face in the Lower Florida was E2 and it became the first production record breaker for the colliery. A newspaper report of July 1965, gave the good news:-

"Parkside Colliery, at Newton-le-Willows, has broken its first output record by becoming the first pit in West Lancashire to achieve 10,000 tons from one face in a week. This '10,000 ton barrier' was smashed by working round the clock on the Lower Florida face while the pit's other face was out of action because of a rock fault. The 10,039 ton target was reached with an output per man shift (OMS) record of 44.2 cwts to break the four year old record held by another North Western pit, Bickershaw Colliery, at Leigh. Pithead output was 12,131 tons from the 280 yard long face equipped with an Anderton shearer loader (ASL) and self advancing roof supports.

Bill Holdsworth commented on the men's achievement:-

"We reached a stage at the end of the week when one shift was competing with another for the best shift output."

The NUM secretary, Frank Pelly, also commented:-

"We all got together to maintain production when one face went out of action because of a major fault. We expect co-operation from the management when we have problems, so it is only right that we co-operate with the management when they have problems. The lads worked as a team."

Visit of Lord Robens - 1970

*Above left to right:
Adam Kuzio, Lord Robens
and Frank King.*

*Right left to right:
Harold Crossland,
Frank Reid, Gerald Eaves
and Lord Robens.*

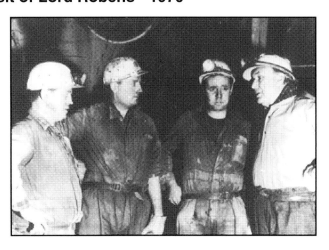

The good news, however, was short lived, because just after the record had been broken the men were gassed out for a fortnight, when there was an outburst of methane in the return. Another disappointment was that E2 was only a short term development face, with a life-span of 8 months. It was the next face in that area, E3, that became the long term money-earner, running for almost 3 years, from 1966 onwards.

After the abandonment of C1 face the main gate was driven down to the far end of No.3 South and that panel of coal was mostly extracted on the rise by C2 and B2 faces, between the years of 1967 and 1971.

In the late 1960's and early 1970's attempts were made to have 3 or 4 faces running at the same time. The colliery production had gone up to over 600,000 tons per year and the manpower was in the region of 1,600 men. The Lower Florida was opened up in No.2 North with series of reasonably successful faces. The series began with D1 in December, 1965, continuing with L2 in 1967, L3 in 1968, L4 in 1969 and L5 in 1973. However, some faces were less successful, with them only lasting a few months. Also, from 1970, a Mid-Area had been developed and series of faces such as L21, L22, L23 and L24 produced coal up to 1974. It was necessary that the colliery be a success and ever increasing pressure must have been applied to the General Manager, Bill Holdsworth. In 1971/72 the production dipped to below 500,000, due to the national dispute, also the manpower reached its greatest level, over 1750 men. The NCB hierarchy must have thought that it was time for a change, so Bill Holdsworth was transferred to Agecroft Colliery in 1972. Bill however still retained his connections with Parkside and the Newton district. It was felt at the time in some quarters that the pit should stop winning trophies and start winning coal, but other sources in the present day state that it is difficult to say how things could have been done better or differently. William Holdsworth left the colliery under a cloud and probably felt that he had failed at Parkside. The new General Manager, Cliff Daniels, was Manager at Golborne Colliery and came to Parkside with some reluctance.

CHANGES.

The new General Manager of Parkside Colliery, Cliff Daniels, was a confident political in-fighter of the first order and he soon made his presence felt at the colliery. He had been very successful at Golborne Colliery and brought many of his technical ideas and innovations to Parkside. Below are his initial thoughts on his transfer:-

"At first I was reluctant to go to Parkside, but eventually took the job on the proviso that I had complete control. My predecessor, Bill Holdsworth, had struggled for years with geological problems and certain strictures applied from Area. When mining had started in the North area, it was found to be extensively faulted and water bearing. Mining conditions were extremely poor, and face life was much less than a year. It was found

impossible to generate sufficient output from the units in production, and impossible to generate replacement units quickly enough."

He had inherited a series of major problems that were inhibiting the development of the colliery: geology, transport and industrial relations. The geological problems were solved by withdrawing from the north side of the pit and concentrating on the south and south-east side. Cliff Daniels also felt that the loco system was inadequate for the colliery and relied too heavily on the state of the locos and their batteries. His thoughts on the subject are:-

Cliff Daniels.

"I pushed through the changeover to conveyors right to the pit bottom, against opposition from some quarters. Conveyor capacity was uprated by increasing belt widths and higher horse-powers, the system was extended to deliver coal into the skip at the pit-bottom. Extending outbye, from 3/19 junction to the pit bottom in three moves, took almost two years to complete, it totally eliminated the dependence on mine cars and the woefully inadequate locomotive system. Substantial bunkerage was built into the circuit. This was probably the most significant, single improvement, ever made at the pit. It ensured that if you could mine the coal, you could get it to the surface. Due to my experience at other collieries I knew that conveyors and bunkerage were very important to maintaining production and that a loco system was not capable of taking a face output at peak times."

With the completion of coal mining in the Lower Florida in No.2 North on L5 face, that section of the pit and No.2 Tippler Station were closed down. From then onwards all coal was brought out along No.3 Horizon to two large bunkers that had been installed at the old No.3 Tippler Station. The only other work that was carried out in No.2 North was S4 face which ran from 1975 till 1977. The majority of the outbye belts were controlled from the surface by a Huwood belt control system. After initial teething problems the system worked well for many years.

In the south of the pit, in the Winwick Area, major developments were being done in the Lower Florida Seam; L15, L23, L18, L14 & L16 were all started in the period between 1972-76. Cliff Daniels recalls one of the faces:-

"L18 became the key to further development in the south-east. We'd turned the face to the right to miss a supposed major fault, but we found it was only a change in ground and after test boring we were able to develop L19 and other good faces in the area."

Other work had been done previously in No.3 North to prove the coal in side of the pit. Alan Sinar, the undermanager, recollects starting at the colliery:-

"When I started at Parkside they were re-opening No.3 North, which had been sealed off for a number of years. In the 1970's, L40 was used as a proving face to indicate the position of the faults in the area. That face proved the ground for other faces in the east side of the pit such as L43, L44, L45 and L46. However the area was highly faulted and coal was difficult to produce."

John Watkins, the undermanager in charge of the North side also recollects his time at Parkside:-

"I was undermanager on the production faces in No.2 & No.3 North. In the late 1970's No.2 North was closed down and production concentrated at No.3. The North side was a completely separate section of the colliery, like a pit of its own. After the eventual closure of No.3 North, I assisted in the development of the Wigan Four Feet faces, W5 and W6, when we really showed our worth."

John Watkins was the longest serving undermanager at Parkside Colliery. He was an outsider to the Lancashire coal-field, having started his career in the Durham coal-field at Houghton Colliery. He later moved to North Staffordshire, working at such pits as Chatterley Whitfield and Florence Collieries, before coming to Parkside.

With the continuing south-easterly direction that the colliery was taking, it became necessary to apply for planning permission from Warrington Council. The General Manager then began a political campaign, aimed at the Warrington and Cheshire councillors, to involve and interest them in the workings and running of a colliery. The pit ran a series of visits accompanied by a talk to allay any fears that they had about subsidence. It was pointed out to them the advantages that a successful colliery could bring to the community, such as employment and prosperity. Cliff Daniels recalls the visits:-

"We entertained the full Warrington Council and then the majority of the Cheshire councillors. They were intelligent people who were genuinely interested in finding out about the colliery and on the whole the exercise was a great success. We got permission to mine under the Orford area with a minimum of fuss."

Visit of Management to Warrington Town Hall.

By the mid-seventies Parkside had become a profitable pit and would continue in that vein, barring strikes, to the end of its days. Negotiations were also going on at that time with local firms to see if they were interested in buying gas from the pit, because of the large amounts being produced and vented at the colliery.

Cliff Daniels became Area Production Manager in 1976 and he left Parkside a much changed place. Although he was General Manager for only 4 years, he had made many long term and fundamental changes to the colliery. Below are his thoughts on the men that he met at the pit:-

"Having outlined the changes in planning, systems and geology, that created the environment for the pit's later successes, it needs to be said that no matter how much capital is invested, the greatest asset at any mine, is the labour force. The major contribution to the success at Parkside came from them. These men had been transferred in from various collieries across the coal field. They were strangers introduced into an unfamiliar

and potentially hostile environment. *They had little success in the early years to boost their morale, but they are a persistent and patient breed of men. They work largely unseen and unsupervised, their loyalty to each other, to their pit and to their manager, generates a spirit of camaraderie that is unique to miners. I was proud to have worked with them. If the pit must close for the lack of market, then it is sad. The miners of Parkside can be justly proud of their achievements."*

The new General Manager, Bertram Dyer, came from Point of Ayr Colliery and before that, Kellingly Colliery.

POTENTIAL.
The changes instituted by Cliff Daniels were developed and improved on by his successor, Bertram Dyer. Production began to increase and by 1979 the pit had achieved its potential and produced over 800,000 tons saleable. The colliery was to consistently achieve this target until the end of its life, baring dispute years. During the late 1970's coal was produced from a large number of faces; at one time reaching 7 in number.

Colliery visit by religious ministers - Bert Dyer 2nd from left front row.

During his time at the colliery Bert Dyer was known as a serious, aloof and cool character. His interests and career were varied, with him being qualified in the mining, economic and naval fields, also being a keen radio ham. He was assisted in mining matters by Jim Wormwell, the most capable and affable of the Deputy Managers.

Below, Bertram Dyer reflects on the differences in working at Kellingley and Parkside:-

"Parkside was sunk at a time of expansion in the industry and was sited to work the seams to the south of the Lancashire coal-field. At the same time a new colliery, Kellingley, was being developed in Yorkshire, at which I was Deputy Manager and the two new mines were broadly very similar in design and layout having twin towers mounted Koepe winders with independent skips and horizon loco tunnels to access the seams. The geological conditions however were very different in that at Kellingley the seams were fairly level and relatively fault free allowing all the production to be got from one seam, the Beeston Seam, from long life faces in good geology. Parkside on the other hand had more inclined seams and was quite heavily faulted in an unpredictable manner. It was also much gassier requiring large quantities of ventilation with a consequent high water gauge to produce it, which because of the high incidence of spontaneous heatings in the Lancashire seams necessitated very careful planning and attention to layout, ventilation and methane extraction systems. Due to the seam gradients and the amount of faulting, output was to be from multi seam working each with its own haulage and transport systems and cross-measure drifts which, unavoidably, was not as efficient or productive as the single seam working at Kellingley."

During his time at Parkside Bertram Dyer spread his net wide, regarding types of coal, in his quest to increase production. The seams being worked in the late 1970's were: Lower Florida, Wigan Four Feet, Ince Six Feet and Trencherbone. He broke the 800,000 ton barrier in 1978/9 with the aid of L19, the longest running face ever at the colliery; it began in May, 1978 and was finally stopped in February, 1984. Below, Alan Sinar remarks about L19:-

"L19 was the best face I encountered at Parkside, even though it went on for a long time both roadways were manageable. L30 started in the same direction but we were informed that it had cross the Motorway at right angles, so the face was turned, much to the detriment of the top road."

The colliery had been limited to 55% extraction to limit subsidence to the motorway system and the Warrington New Town development. Ray Bolton, the colliery surveyor, explains:-

"It was decided to limit all future faces to 1200 metre runs and stabilise the take, keeping all the faces vertically the same. L30 was running at the time and it was turned to bring it in line with the proposed extraction from other seams. The faces were taken in an alternative panel then pillar system, with the Ince Six Feet being two panels in front of the Wigan Four Feet faces. This stopped any strains on the surface strata."

Due to the large amounts of methane being produced and vented by the colliery, investigations were made into whether any of the local companies would be interested in purchasing gas on a long term basis.

In August, 1978, the NCB signed a contract with Crosfields Ltd., of Bank Quay, Warrington, to supply methane from Parkside to the company's boilers via a pipeline. The resulting pipeline was laid alongside the main roads running from Newton to Warrington. At Parkside an unused plot of land between the methane extraction plant and the coal preparation plant was converted into the methane sales installation. The work was completed by 1980 and cost approximately £4 million, which was recouped within 2 years.

The initial contract guaranteed a yearly supply of 7.5 million therms of gas and the contract was revised to supply over 12 million therms from June, 1983. The methane contract for Parkside Colliery was the largest ever negotiated by the Coal Board up to that date. However, the money was never attributed to the pit, with it being paid directly to area, much to the aggravation of the men. Norman Harrison, the Gas Sales Engineer, recalls his time when he was in charge of Methane Sales:-

"I was already employed at the colliery as a ventilation officer, when my boss, Geoff Hodkinson, suggested that I be put in sole charge of methane sales. It was obvious from the start that the minimum figure could be easily beaten and our output quickly increased to an average of 12 million therms. In the year 1986/87 we earned a clear profit of £2.64 million from the gas sales to Crosfields. They were well satisfied with the contract because of the reduction in cost and the guarantee of supply. Other collieries in the district did not bother to maintain their supply on backshifts and weekends. It was due to me being allowed to concentrate solely on the sales aspect that produced such large profits. At the colliery I was backed up by an excellent boring team and supported by my ventilation colleagues. Due to our extensive boring programme we had a multitude of holes to draw gas from. Even when districts were sealed up the best of the drainage holes were left connected to the system. Some of the holes that were drilled in the 1960's were still in use at the end of the pit's life. It was a very satisfying job and I was proud to be involved in the project."

During the late 1970's it became obvious that the further south the Parkside workings went, the better the strata was, with less faults and easier gradients. The General Manager, Bertram Dyer, recollects:-

"As the workings moved south from the shafts conditions improved and in the late 70's a decision was made to work faces to the south towards Orford. The gradient was kinder and the faulting patterns which

by now were predictable allowed long life high production faces and it was at this time that the annual saleable output exceeded 800,000 tons for the first time and the colliery became profitable. With hindsight one can say that had the shafts been sited one mile due south of where they were sunk then the colliery would have reached profitability much sooner and been a much easier pit to manage."

Bertram Dyer moved from Parkside to Victoria Colliery in 1981, and from there took early retirement. The new General Manager came from Golborne Colliery and returned to where he had spent the majority of his career.

THE RETURN.

The year 1981 saw the return to Parkside of one of its most familiar and respected officials. Francis Patrick Reid was appointed General Manager in August of that year and holds a unique record in the Lancashire coal-field. He has held every mining official position at the same colliery, from shot-firer to General Manager. Frank Reid started work at Wigan Junction and was employed at Robin Hill, Bickershaw, Parsonage and Golborne throughout a distinguished career of 35 years.

Sheila Worthington, Frank Reid and Sister Fish.

During his tenure as General Manager, Frank Reid, carried out the costliest improvement programme since the building of the colliery. It was to completely change the colliery from a multi-face pit to production from two units in the Wigan Four Feet and Ince Six Feet seams. Geological problems had led to the northern area being closed down and most of the work was concentrated in the South and Mid areas. The manpower was sadly reduced to almost half its number, but with the improvements made, the production stayed the same and then increased to the pit's greatest level.

Throughout the 1980's the colliery was upgraded on the mining, mechanical and electrical fronts. It was felt that certain sections of the mine had become old fashioned and out-dated. Millions of pounds were invested at the pit to bring it up to the standards of a modern colliery. Below are a selection of the major investments that were carried out:-

(1) Both main ventilating fans were changed to improve ventilation in the new Wigan Mines Access project.

(2) The No.2 tower was strengthened because of the higher water gauge caused by the increase in ventilation.

(3) The No.1 Shaft winding system was changed from two individual winders to one winder and two cages.

(3) A completely new compressed air pipe range was installed down No.1 Shaft.

(4) A new surface control centre was built incorporating the MINOS conveyor control and environmental monitoring systems.

(5) Manriding was improved by a new 15 mph rope manrider from No.2 Horizon to the East Winwick Area.

(6) Diesel powered Free Steered Vehicles (FSVs) were introduced to improve Material handling at the faces.

(7) The surface Liner Train was installed to provide a quicker 'merry go round' loader for the British Rail locomotives.

(8) A Filter Press Plant costing over #1 million was installed to improve the quality of filter cake - a profitable by-product from the CPP.

(9) A Non-inclined Strata Bunker (NISBI) was installed to improve bunkerage because of the expected increase in output from the south-side.

Alan Schofield, the last Electrical Engineer, gives an indication of some of the technical details in his 'electrical engineering revolution.':-

"During the 1980's large investments were provided to enable Parkside Colliery to be competitive using the latest state of the art Technology.

Manpower intensive local controlled coal clearance systems were modernised using computer technology and transducers. This enabled remote control of 30 conveyors from a new MINOS Control Room.

Using a dedicated computer and such State of the Art technology as Fidescos, BMI methane detectors and temperature transducers, the mine environment safety was enhanced by continuous monitoring provided by these computers.

Mechanisation of coal faces and developments to improve productivity increased power demand and saturated the 3300v system.

Installation and commissioning of a new 6600v distribution system underground ensured the outputs could be supplied with electricity effectively.

The 1960's Mercury Arc Winders were becoming obsolete and therefore entering their life cycle limits. Modernisation of the Winders took place with each of the three Winders being modified to Thyristor technology."

The major decision at the colliery in the eighties was to abandon coal production in the Lower Florida and Crombouke seams and concentrate on two heavy duty units in the south area of the colliery working the Ince Six Feet and Wigan Four Feet. The £12 million scheme included two mile long access tunnels, improved man/materials/coal conveying systems, 2,000 tonnes of extra bunkerage and the new ventilating fans previously mentioned. The colliery manpower was reduced, due to less faces being worked, to a level of approximately 1000 men. By 1986, W11, the first of the heavy duty units was running, and appeared regularly in the top ten National face league. Other good production faces followed in the Ince and Wigan seams, with the colliery becoming one of the most profitable in the district.

The decision to abandon work in the Lower Florida was taken by Frank Reid, the General Manager. It had been the most extensively worked seam at the colliery, but had always encountered problems with floor lift. The new developments that were going on at the time in the Lower Florida were meeting with levels of 1 metre of floor lift after 30 metres of drivage. No further work was done in that seam after L33, but it was thought that mining could be done in it in the future.

The year 1984 saw the retirement of one of the pit's longest serving and influential officials. John Connaughton, the undermanager, had been connected with all the major changes that had gone on at the colliery. He was a fierce, aggressive and dedicated character, always on the move, never still, but highly respected by other officials.

One great disadvantage of the reduction in manpower was the loss of a large amount of mining expertise. The majority of the men that took early retirement in the mid eighties had spent all of their working lives in mining and the loss of their experience was a great blow to the pit. A policy that the Coal Board was using at that time was to guarantee a job to any young man who had a parent at the pit. Due to the high unemployment in the area the colliery became flooded out with relatives, or what was termed at the pit 'Dads and Lads'.

In August 1989, the general manager, Frank Reid, took early retirement, at the time that the colliery was achieving its greatest production level. He had been involved with the colliery since its beginning and was sadly missed by some of his friends and associates. The new general manager, Michael Ramsey, came from Shirebrook Colliery, where he had been deputy manager.

John Watkins and Charles Huggard on W11's face.

NEW BLOOD.

The last general manager of Parkside Colliery was the youngest to hold the post, being only 35 when he took over. Other young men appeared at that time and the management team took on a youthful appearance. It was felt that this young team would take the colliery through the nineties and into the next century. During his tenure as the general manager the colliery had its greatest years, production staying consistently high throughout the early 1990's. However, at that time British Coal were attempting to enforce ever more stricter Health and Safety regulations and this caused resentment amongst the men. The wearing of special safety equipment was implemented, and fines imposed for any misdemeanour. These rules created a feeling of unrest and uncertainty in the workforce, thinking that it was part of a dirty tricks campaign.

Michael Ramsey.

In 1990/91 the colliery achieved its highest saleable production, mining 981,749 tonnes of coal, just 5 days output away from the magic million. The faces that produced the record were: S32, W32 and S33.

Throughout the early nineties Parkside looked forward to a secure future, having reserves that would carry it well into the next century. No further capital outlay was required during the next ten years and the colliery had a safe market for the major part of its production. The Coal Prep Plant had solved the Ash content,

Chlorine content and Moisture content problems that had dogged them for a number of years. Fiddler's Ferry Power Station was well satisfied with Parkside's coal and commented on the fact many times. However, storm clouds loomed ahead for Parkside, as well as other British Coal pits.

ENDGAME.

The last year of the colliery's life was a hard and difficult one; hard for the workforce battling to achieve better results and difficult due to pressures on the colliery and industry as a whole. Additionally, the last year saw the workforce in dispute over the sacking of two men for illegal manriding at the mine. Jeff Booth, the colliery deputy manager, describes how much pressure the colliery was under:-

"The colliery management were well aware of the pressure that the government were applying to British Coal. Our major competitor was imported fuel and the need to be more competitive in the market place. It was a time of great upheaval in the coal industry and I'm still sure the men did not fully appreciate the severity of the situation until it was too late. It was most unfortunate for the mine that a dispute occurred at this time but Parkside had to produce more coal, more efficiently and still maintain its high safety standards."

Geological problems added to the misery of that final 12 months. Following the influx of men from the nearby Bickershaw complex and the Area meeting in July, giving notice to the pit for the need to produce more coal, the colliery had the worst month ever in its history. Both faces experienced water problems, something that Parkside had never encountered for 10 years. This, together with unrest in the workforce led to a downturn in production instead of the required upturn. The men felt frustrated with the situation and the many rumours at the pit inflamed an already volatile situation. The bad luck continued throughout August and at the area meeting on the 17th the axe inevitably fell; there was to be no further use for Parkside colliery after March 31st 1993.

It was a sad day at the colliery and the majority of the men put the blame firmly at the government's door. They believed that there was a 'witch hunt' against the British miner stretching as far back as the strikes in the 1970's. The government believed that miners could not be trusted to supply the fuel for the country and alternative supplies were to be used.

For two days the pit was in a state of shock, with even the 'shut it now' and 'put lid on' brigade silenced, struck dumb by their own words. At first, the pit carried on as if nothing had happened, cables being installed and

W31's District

*Above: Ian Handley, Jeff Booth, Jimmy Frampton, David Wolfendale,
David Grayson, Graham Kirby, Peter Valentine and Carl Rimatis.*

Below: John Bennett, Steve Rourke, Mick Newton, Gary Grimshaw and Peter Kevill.

machinery sent underground for the new S35's face. However, within a week all development had ceased and the colliery concentrated its work on the last two units; W31 and the soon to be started, S35. S35's face was a new face costing in excess of £6 million. The face started production in October 1992 initially having problems getting away but having all the indications of being capable of producing the goods. It was not to be however, the face being stopped before it could establish itself and cause any embarrassment. The potential of S35 is outlined by Jeff Booth:-

"S35 was the last in production at the pit in the Ince 6ft seam. Its full potential was never realised. I think the face could have produced good results."

Jeff Booth began his career in the early 1970's at Florence and then Hem Heath collieries before transferring to Sutton Manor in 1984. He was in charge of the reconstruction of Sutton Manor between 1984 and 1986, after which he transferred to Parkside where he worked until its closure and left the industry. His thoughts of Parkside are summed up:-

"Parkside was a pit with difficult mining conditions and it was a credit to the men that they worked it at all."

Of his time in the industry he says:-

"Of the twenty years I did in the coal industry I can say I enjoyed every minute. It has been a hard time but in any industry, especially the mining industry, it was the people working in it that made the industry what it was. Once the workforce is taken away the pit's soul is lost.

The important lesson to be learnt about the demise of the industry is the importance of the market. No market means no industry."

The government announcement on the 13th October hit the coal-fields and the country like a thunderbolt, with 31 pits and 31,000 jobs to go immediately. The resulting furore ran through the country like a forest fire. MPs on both sides of the house objected in the strongest terms to the government's handling of the situation. It was to cause the biggest climb down by the present government and should have resulted in the resignation of the minister involved, but he clung on to his job like a pit bull terrier.

At pit level the majority of the men were laid off and the remainder were termed the care and maintenance team. This group of men were to maintain the fabric of the mine in case it returned to production. Throughout the long months the men waited to hear their fate and see whether their livelihood would be destroyed by an uncaring government. The more ambitious men left in trickles to a secure future without the problems of the coal industry. As the months went by British Coal expected the trickle to turn into a rush for the 'wedge', but at Parkside it did not happen. Some scrawls appeared around the pit: 'Give me the wedge now', referring to the amount of money they were due to. However, there was no great rush for money at Parkside, as happened at other pits in the country. The majority of the men held the line and even six months into the care and maintenance fiasco, there were still approximately 500 men signing on daily. In April the care and maintenance team was reduced to 60% of its size, and then in May the BACM personnel were reduced to a more sensible level.

Care and Maintenance Team:
Back row left to right: Peter Prescot, Derek Gibson and Alan Edwards.
Front row left to right: Cliff Graham, Peter Hartley, John Beech and Lionel Nabakow.

Reminiscing became the favourite pastime at the colliery, during the long boring days of waiting for a decision to be made by British Coal. Tales of years gone by were related by the pit comics, some stretched and exaggerated for the maximum effect. Smuggled in dart boards became heavily used, and some of the men reached championship level.

At the end, the news of the closure came with a certain amount of relief, the men becoming sick of rumour and conjecture.

Employment of British Coal workmen at Parkside Colliery, barring a few management exceptions, finished on the 4th of June, 1993. The majority of the remaining men on the books signed up for their redundancy and lump sum. It was termed voluntary redundancy but it was only voluntary with threat. If the men had not signed, part of their lump sum would have been withdrawn. The last days at the colliery left a bad taste in the mouth because of the loss of many old friends and colleagues. The care and maintenance team were taken on by Davy Mining, a private company that had mysteriously appeared at the colliery that week. The colliery was to be put up for sale to the private sector and the fabric of the colliery was to be maintained until this offer was completed. By September no bids had been received for Parkside and therefore it was to be closed as soon as possible.

Davy Mining carried on with the Care and Maintenance of the colliery, expecting to get the closure contract as well. Their hopes were soon dashed by the intervention of the Women Against Pit Closures group, who had established themselves at the bottom of the colliery road. Women Against Pit closure groups began to appear at other collieries in December 1992, as a protest against the numbers of pit closures that were occurring in the country. They appeared first at Markham Main Colliery and then at Houghton and Grimethorpe Collieries. At Parkside they appeared in January 1993, when a small caravan was sited on the grass verge at the entrance. The women soon attracted many followers in their valiant but futile attempt to save the colliery. Marches, protests, meetings, blockades, break-ins and rallies were their main weapons, even attracting the support of a gay group, much to the amusement of the local pit-men. In October 1993, their repeated break-ins into restricted parts of the colliery resulted in British Coal 'pulling the plug' at Parkside. All power was switched off to the pit and Parkside was abandoned. The main ventilating fan, which had run for over 30 years, barring breakdowns, was stopped, never to run again. On that day in October Parkside Colliery died an ignominious death unworthy of the achievements of the men who had staffed it throughout its short life.

DEMOLITION.

The company that got the contract for the demolition of Parkside was Ling Demolition from Kent, who moved onto the site in May 1994. British Coal probably wished to use a firm which had no local connections and therefore no involvement in the feelings of the locality. The company had first to contend with the WAPC group, who were still encamped at the pit, when they started work at the colliery. The women carried on their protest for a few more months finally giving up their campaign in August 1994. Besides the demolition team there were British Coal staff on site to oversee the safety aspects of the work. One of them, Mick Hibbert, had the unenviable task of knocking down the place where he had worked for a number of years:-

"One of the saddest days was when they demolished my old office. All those memories of planning, discussing and arguing went with one swipe of a JCB."

Over 100,000 tons of limestone were used to fill the shafts and the surface buildings were systematically demolished one by one. What had taken hundreds of men years to construct was demolished by 15 men in a matter of months. Graham Carr, ex-Parkside drivage man and ace photographer, was allowed on site by British Coal to record the proceedings. His thoughts on the many visits he made are a heartfelt epitaph to the colliery:-

"To see a colliery site razed to the ground is for some too much to bear. Memories are all that is left for the lads to talk about, but what I personally realise is, whatever the site of Parkside looks like in years to come nobody can change what exists underground. The very nature of the

Graham Carr on S35's face.

earth beneath your feet has been altered, the pit bottoms along with all the machinery left underground will remain as they are now for many years to come. I am more fortunate than some in one respect, I can look back through the hundreds of photographs that I took underground at the pit, and with this in mind I decided I would photograph the demolition of the colliery. Having sought permission from the group director, Brian Arrowsmith, I was granted access to the site. The first thing to go was the rapid loader along with the engineering workshops, where the shaft fill aggregates were to be stockpiled. Next to go was the landsale and following that, the coal preparation plant was stripped of asbestos and subsequently demolished. Further visits to the pit saw the powerhouse, gasometer and press-plant go and during one such visit I photographed the shafts being filled. It was then that the full horror of what was happening actually hit home. All the people around me were from different parts of the country, I felt alienated at my own pit. I could not expect these people to show any emotion, to them it was just another job. The ropes and guide rods had been dropped down the shaft a month or so before filling had started, it was at this point that there was no going back, that was the end!"

By the first week in October 1994 little remained except the towers standing in a sea of rubble. They were weakened at their bases and the charges were set for their final demolition at 10am on October 9th.

Hundreds of people came from near and far to witness the last death throes of Parkside Colliery. Ex-workmen, press, television, onlookers and the just plain curious gathered around the colliery, many of them to take a last picture of a falling giant. The charges went off precisely on time and Parkside winding towers, which had dominated the Newton skyline for over 30 years, disappeared in a matter of seconds. No.1 tower fell gracefully to its knees before falling on its face, but No.2 fell on its back like a broken man. After the dust cleared there was nothing left but a pile of broken concrete, twisted steelwork and memories. Ugly they may have been, but they were also distinctive, visible for miles around, a welcoming homecoming symbol for the locality.

Ling Demolition were pleased with their day's work, because everything had gone well from their point of view, but elsewhere there were quite a few tears shed on that cold morning in October. The last deep coal mine in the old Lancashire coal-field had gone never to return. It was the final chapter in a once proud Lancashire industry that spanned hundreds of years and employed millions of men.

The author and the ruins of the main offices.

Demolition of Winding Towers.

Part Two

Life at the Colliery

"Putting John on a diet"

Left to right: Mick Corns, Brian Pelly, Ian Abbot, John Genner, Sylvia Pye, Sister Fish, Ray Brown, Phil Steel and Derek Bainbridge.

WORK AND PLAY.

Working underground at a colliery is one of the most difficult forms of employment available to the British working man. It can be dirty, dark, wet, uncomfortable, dangerous, dusty and hot. Of course there are equally bad conditions in other industries, but a miner, from the time he goes down the pit, is trapped in his work environment until he ascends. Other types of worker can step back and take a break, even if it is only for a few minutes, but not a miner. This tended to breed into the majority of miners a different personality and humour from other workers. Their humour was looked on as black and cruel in some quarters. They worked together, sometimes in dangerous conditions, drank together and lived in close communities, hence the term 'pit village.' At Parkside the men came from different townships, but eventually they developed the close friendship and rivalry of men working under adverse conditions.

The simple fact that Parkside drew its workforce from the closure of over 11 collieries produced a varied workforce. Three of the local towns, Wigan, St. Helens and Leigh, provided eighty per cent of the manpower during the pit's life. These towns, even though they are closely situated, have very distinct characteristics and dialects. Another factor that caused rivalry is that Wigan, St. Helens and Leigh are rugby league towns having very passionate supporters at the pit. All kinds of remarks, threats and even fights on Monday morning resulted from the feelings between winners and losers. Such a large number of men being drafted in from different collieries did cause certain problems. Frank King can still remember some of the problems that occurred:-

"The best example was the animosity between the Chisnall Hall men and the Robin Hill men which went back to the days when they were at their own collieries. The men wanted to keep together because they trusted old friends and associates. It took a good few years before they turned into Parkside men."

Stan Horsfield recollects the part he played in some of these internal arguments:-

"In the early days of the pit's life the majority of the men came from a series of closed collieries and it did cause some problems. They were used to different working practices and life styles. The men tried to retain their own identities and stay in their own groups. It took three or four years to weld them into the Parkside workforce. One major difficulty was with the holiday period. At that time we were working with men from twelve areas that had different school holidays, wakes weeks and the added problem of working wives. At first we rotated the holiday fortnight to satisfy the men

from these different areas. Another thing that had to be rotated was the union branch meeting place. The Chorley men were always saying, 'We're always bloody travelling to St. Helens.' We finally decided to have a 'once and for all ballot' on the holidays and meeting place. It was decided to hold the branch meetings at Platt Bridge Labour Club and have the last week in July and first week in August as the pit holidays."

Pit language can be described in some circles as colourful. Swearing was used at all levels in the coal industry, from the area management down to the lowest paid worker. It was used to register anger, rage, surprise, pain and joy. Just like the famous Watergate affair with its 'expletive deleted', if all the expletives were deleted from some pit-men's language there would be very little left. Pit swear-words can be listed in certain groups: the Lord's name, colloquial descriptions of sexual intercourse, types of private parts and casting doubt on a person's lineage, or a combination.

Serious injury and death go hand in hand with the daily work of a miner. They had to be vigilant at all times because of the underground environment and working conditions. The accident rate in British mines had been reduced to a low level through the endeavours of the Inspectorate backed up by the NUM and the majority of management. However, a coal mine is still a dangerous place of work and accidents do occur. At Parkside there were 15 deaths during the life of the pit, and many serious accidents. Some of the men who were killed are listed below, young men as well as old, showing that accidental death is no respecter of age.

Stan Moyers - Assistant Mech. Engineer.
Jack Gardener - Faceworker.
Lenny Partington - Conveyor Attendant.
Robert Young - Linesman.
Jack Taylor - Faceworker.
Frank Martin - Cutterman.
Paul McGuinness - Deputy.
Arnold Nicholson - Foreman Contractor.

Near misses also occurred at the colliery, men escaping with their lives only to lose a limb or suffer some other serious disability. The luckiest escape occurred in 1983 in one of the shafts. The local and national newspapers were full of reports about the miraculous escape of Henry (Harry) Daniels, a Parkside Shaftsman. He had been carrying out routine maintenance in No.2 shaft when, after uncoupling his safety harness he slipped from the top of the cage and fell into the shaft. The two men working with him, Derek Gibson and Ian Lindsay, at first thought that he was a goner, but were relieved to hear him shout on the communication system that he was all right. On first toppling into the shaft Harry had grabbed the nearest rope to him and, thankfully, slid down to the next landing, over 100 metres below. The resulting burns meant that he required extensive skin grafts to his hands.

Another lucky escape concerning shaft work occurred in 1986 during the installation of a new compressed air range in No.1 shaft. Three men, Alexander Atherton (Sandy), Derek Gibson (Gibbo) and Ian Lindsay, were fitting a pipe bracket to the shaft wall above No.1 Horizon when the 92 pipes that had already been installed snapped off and collapsed down the shaft, severing a balance rope and completely destroying the pit bottom and steelwork. Each of the pipes was 15 foot long, 16 inches in diameter and weighed 3/4 of a ton. The three men had to be left on the cage for over five hours until the emergency winder arrived from Stoke.

NUM

Throughout the pit's lifetime the NUM was well established and represented by its officials. They were men from ordinary backgrounds, but at times had the power to shake governments. Some of them were quite famous in their day: Frank Pelly, the first secretary, Stan Horsfield, secretary for 10 years, Mick Noonan, Frank King, Bill Shaw, Bill Ormshaw, Tommy Meadows, Jimmy Holmes, Billy Pye and Jimmy Hughes all played their part in their own battles with management. Frank King, who later became the area union president, remembers Frank Pelly well:-

"Frank Pelly was a well respected and well established union man of the old order who was conversant with common law and accident cases. It was reputed that he was the best in the area in this field."

Left to right: Lord Robens, Frank Pelly, Stan Horsfield and Alf Downes.

The second NUM secretary was Stan Horsfield who came to Parkside from Lyme Pits in 1964. He was initially trained as a loco-driver and then was offered a temporary position in the medical room because Alf Downes was off sick. He became a full time attendant when it was thought that the pit required 24 hour cover. Stan later went back underground as a methane borer installing the large network of methane extraction pipes. He was a long-term member of the very successful Parkside first-aid team from the 1960's until 1972. His interest in the NUM was rewarded over the years when he became firstly a committee member, then branch treasurer in 1966 and branch secretary in 1971, after the retirement of Frank Pelly. In 1981 he was elected as NUM Area Agent, trouble-shooting at all of the remaining pits in the area, a position that he held until his retirement in 1992. Stan Horsfield was succeeded at Parkside by Mick Noonan who had come to the pit from Lea Green colliery and was to be secretary for over twelve years retiring in 1993. He was secretary during the most traumatic period in the coal industry, having to contend with the 'great strike' of 1984 and the destruction of the industry in the 1990's. After Mick Noonan the secretary's duties were carried out by Paul Hardman until the pit closed.

Two of the union men previously mentioned, Tommy Meadows and Jimmy Holmes, were employed at Parkside from the development days till the last years of the pit's life. They began at the colliery in 1963 as 16 year old haulage lads. Both of them developed their mining skills and became face charge-hands in the 1980's. The two men were always involved in the success of the colliery and later in their careers they became union officials.

PIT VISITS.

Pit visits to the colliery by groups, societies or the general public really began in the 1970's. There had been visits before but they were usually limited to NCB and government officials, who were interested in where their money was being invested. There were three levels of entertainment provided after the visits ranging from sandwiches and pies to steaks and wine, depending on the persons involved. Ron Silver was the main organiser of the trips:-

"Derek Taylor and I organised the trips for many of the Warrington Councillors. They were wined and dined and given the best of treatment. The Mayor was so pleased that he invited a group from the pit to Warrington Town Hall for a luncheon. The trips later snowballed to include councillors from other parts of Cheshire."

Visits became established on a regular weekly basis, with many local groups taking advantage of the offer of an underground trip. Over the years many famous people have visited the colliery, MPs like Anthony Wedgwood Benn, Fred Lee, Roy Mason, John Moore, John Evans came, as did coal board chiefs such as Lord Robens, Lord Ezra and Lord Haslam, and

Above:
Visit of Tony Benn MP
Left to right: Tom Liptrot,
Bill Bullen, John Connaughton,
Tony Benn, Cliff Daniels,
Jim Wormwell and John Watkins.

Right: Bill Holdsworth with a
party of Bolivian visitors.

personalities like Colin Welland and Anna Ford. Groups from the Rotary and Round Table organisations, the police, shop groups, coal dealers, nurses, reporters and students normally made their visits on Thursday evening. There are many stories about the visits, some more amusing than others. Ron Silver relates three of his highlights:-

"On one of the Marks & Spencer's trips a young lady collapsed exhausted half-way up the face. Our first intention was to get her off the face so that we could help her. Her desperate comment was 'I can't move an inch, my head hurts, my back hurts and my knickers are full of coal'."

"One famous female dignitary who visited us came without proper clothes, so we loaned her some pit drawers and a jacket. I believe the drawers were raffled off in the baths afterwards."

"The police were always taken to the nearest face to the pit bottom, somewhere in the mid-area. However, one of them commented that it was easy down the pit and wondered why pitmen were paid so much. I'm afraid their visits were never the same again and they certainly came up tired."

Foreign groups from as far afield as China have appeared and enjoyed their visit to the pit. However, one Iraqi group from the Vulcan Works were most upset when, during their underground trip, they found a chalked notice over a junction saying that the Ayatollah had built it. They were most disconcerted until they were informed that it was the nickname for one of the officials.

One of the general managers, who will remain nameless, thought things were going a bit too far when a request came from Winwick Hospital for an inmates' visit. His comment was that, 'we have enough in the management team.' A visit to Parkside Colliery was graphically described by Brian Baker, a local reporter :-

"It was to have been a boys' night out for myself and a few friends, one of whom is an assistant engineer at Parkside Colliery, Newton-le-Willows who offered to show us around. What I had in mind was a quick look round, maybe a ride on one of those little trains and back up again for the few hours drinking time left on the clock. If I'd have known what was in store about 1,500ft underground I'd have suggested something more sedate, like a crash course in free-fall parachuting.

Parkside is one of our most modern pits, built in the 1960's and the biggest in the North West. But for all the modern facilities, like the giant coal cutters that rip coal out of the seams by the ton, it still has to be worked by men who are prepared to spend nearly a third of their daily lives in places which the human race was not designed to inhabit.

The reality of this does not strike home until you are scrunched up in a box-sized space, a pit prop painfully digging in your back, your helmeted head jammed up against the roof. You are eating and breathing coal dust. You eyes are gummed up with it; your hair is matted with it. You are blowing hard and the sweat on your body drying cold after what seems like miles of scurrying, scrambling and crawling through interminable galleries. You ache from head to foot. Even your eyelashes ache. Then, somewhere close at hand, there is a crashing rumble of a roof fall and you make peace with God, waiting for a section of Cheshire or of Greater Manchester County to drop on you. As tour highlights go, this is only surpassed by the heart-stopping terror of the conveyor belt ride.

After a fifth or sixth forced march we grouped uncertainly round a wooden platform and a sign that stated 'Board here'. The belt was zipping along merrily and I wondered when they were going to stop it so we could take our seats. But like time and tide, the Parkside Colliery conveyor belt waits for no man. You climb onto the platform. Facing you, above the belt, is a sort of wooden cradle, loosely fashioned on the old village ducking stool. You waddle onto the cradle, it tilts suddenly and with top teeth drawing blood from lower lip you dive headlong, bouncing once or twice and lie there amongst the remnants of the last load of coal, whimpering hysterically. I'm not sure how I got off eventually, though there is a blurred memory of somehow teetering to my feet, and lunging frantically for a wooden rail and a strong helping hand. Other memories will live forever:-

Staggering and lurching towards a cluster of bobbing lamps to hear a band of faceworkers tunefully singing 'Happy Birthday' to one of their mates.

A man with the shoulders of a bull and hands like dinner plates delicately preparing to take a tiny pinch of snuff - the miner's equivalent of a sly drag.

The incredible speed of the drop in the cage which turned me deaf and the incredible speed of the return journey which restored my hearing.

After it was all over, the best shower I've had in my life at the pit head baths, watching about five quid's worth of coal being sluiced off me.

I will never, ever, go down a mine again. But if any one ever suggests in my presence that miners are idle or greedy or overpaid or holding the country to ransom, I shall probably spit in his eye."

After October 1992, during the care and maintenance period, there was a change in the normal weekly pit visit. Some of the colliery Overmen, namely Ray Hall and Stuart Hibbert, began to organise more visits for their families and friends. By 1993, there were 3 visits a week at the pit and the men began to term it "Ray Hall's Tourist Board." The families and friends who came were amazed with their new insight into pit life and the lectures by

Ray at various points during the tour were cheered and applauded by any pit-men in the vicinity.

However, in April 1993, all visits were stopped, as in all British Coal collieries, with the 4 day sit-in by Ann Scargill at Parkside. On Thursday 8th April four members of the Women Against Pit Closures went underground at Parkside in a party of fifteen people on one of the organised visits. At the end of the tour the four staged a 'sit-in' at the pit bottom, carrying on their protest for over five days. Some of the care and maintenance team felt sorry for the group and sneaked water and provisions past the sentries. Ken Pennington, the onsetter, claimed that he was kissed by all four of them after taking down some perfume!

BUSES.

The manpower of such a large industrial unit, like Parkside, was gathered from many of the local towns in the district. Parkside was never a village pit like many of the other collieries in Britain, so the men had to be transported great distances to their work place. Ron Silver, who was personnel manager from 1974-92, had the job of organising the bus transport:-

"At one time we had as many as 12 bus routes into the colliery and each route had to be worked out to pick up the maximum number of men."

Many of the routes were highly complicated, with the times booked down to the minute at each stop. A good example of one of the routes is shown below:-

Punchbowl (Atherton) - 05.35
Bull and Butcher (Hindley Green) - 05.38
The Swan (Hindley Green) - 05.41
Victoria Inn (Hindley Green) - 05.42
Borsdale Avenue (Hindley) - 05.44
Bird I'th Hand (Hindley) - 05.48
Ince Bar (Squirrel Inn) - 05.51
Bird I'th Hand (Ince Green Lane) - 05.53
Black Diamond (Lower Ince) - 05.54
Walmesley Arms (Spring View) - 05.57
King William (Platt Bridge) - 06.00
Platt Bridge Legion - 06.02
Bamfurlong Hotel - 06.04
Riding Lane (Stubshaw) - 06.06
Rams Head (Stubshaw) - 06.07
Caledonian Hotel (Ashton) -06.09
Red Lion (Ashton) - 06.12
Robinsons (Ashton) -06.15
Pied Bull (Newton) - 06.21
Parkside - 06.25

The above list does not necessarily mean that colliers congregate near pubs, but they are usually the most prominent buildings on a street.

At its peak nearly 1800 men worked at the pit. The majority of them came from the mining areas in the district, but others came from further afield. The townships which contributed to the Parkside workforce with the numbers of men from each are shown in the following list. It gives a clear indication of the influence the pit had in the area and shows what a great loss it was to the surrounding towns:-

Southport (1)	Burscough (3)	Upholland (2)	Leyland (20)
Shevington (12)	Billinge (7)	Orrell (7)	Pemberton (47)
Preston (1)	Coppull (106)	Standish (45)	Chorley (64)
Blackrod (9)	Adlington (20)	Aspull (8)	Horwich (2)
Westhoughton (4)	Blackburn (2)	Bolton (4)	Farnworth (3)
Salford (2)	Manchester (2)	Tyldesley (37)	Atherton (91)
Hindley (68)	Leigh (124)	Lowton (17)	Culcheth (4)
Golborne (44)	Abram (12)	Platt Bridge (14)	Bamfurlong (3)
Ince (45)	Wigan (172)	Bryn (34)	Ashton (79)
Haydock (188)	Newton (125)	Earlestown (16)	Burtonwood (9)
Warrington (16)	Parr (93)	St.Helens (89)	Rainhill (2)
Widnes (3)	Liverpool (3)	Birkenhead (2)	

This survey was carried out when the manpower was 1643. It showed that the workforce were drawn from an area of over 900 sq. miles.

A MINE OF TALENT.

Parkside Colliery, over the years, has proved to be a veritable mine of talent. In sport, entertainment, glamour and literary fields the colliery has employed many people who should be proud of their achievements. Most of the activities were financially supported by the active welfare fund organised by the union. Parkside boasted a successful First Aid Team, a competitive Safety Quiz Team, a Golf Society, a Rugby Team, a Chess Club, a Shooting Club, a Fishing Club and a famous Choir.

In the sporting field the athletic expertise present is shown by its Marathon men. Parkside has employed 8 men who have run full marathons and a further number that have succeeded at the half marathon distance. For sheer numbers the pit record must go to Jeff Gorton, the deputy Mechanical Engineer, who has run 22 full and thirty half marathons.

In second place is John Irwin, the assistant Electrical Engineer, who has completed 14 full and 35 half marathons. John was a late starter to the running game at the age of 40, being unknowingly entered for a race by his daughter. Since then he has become a stalwart member of the Sutton Harriers Athletic Club.

The next runner in our list is Dave Berry, the electrician, who has worked at the colliery since 1968. He has completed 8 full and 15 half marathons for Multiple Sclerosis.

Next in the marathon stakes is Bob Selby, the colliery Winder, who has completed 5 full and 5 half marathons. Bob has always been interested in fitness, being a successful boxer during his National Service. For many years Bob has supported the Newton Boys Club and the majority of his sponsorship money went to that cause. Bob's greatest claim to fame was that he was nearly killed by John Conteh, the famous boxer. He had been called out of semi-retirement to test this new young boxer from Liverpool with the remark: 'You'll be alright Bob, just give him a few rounds and teach him a lesson.' Bob remembers: 'There was flurry of blows and I found myself on the deck. I decided not to get up so as to save him further punishment.'

The most spectacular of the marathon feats must be attributed to Neil Williams, the colliery mechanic, who has run in both the London and New York marathons. Neil is known for being a zany and extrovert character, having travelled the world in pursuit of the unusual.

Senior management have also played their part in the running stakes. Surface Superintendent, Winston Hodgkinson, has completed 3 marathons, two in the aid of charity. Jeff Booth, the Deputy Manager, weighs in with 1 full and 32 half marathons and Michael Ramsey, the General Manager, the sprinter of the group, chips in with 12 half marathons.

The Parkside Colliery First Aid Team became well known, respected and feared by other teams in the Mining, St. John Ambulance and Open First Aid Competitions. It was formed in 1964 and won the Area Competition for twelve years from 1965-77. In 1970, 1971 and 1974 they won the National First Aid Competition, becoming the top team in the coal industry. The spectacular trophy for that competition was the Mitchell Hedges Trophy; a large oval-shaped, solid silver trophy weighing 95lbs. It was designed and made in 1815 and was kindly given to the coal industry by the explorer Mitchell Hedges, hence its name. Initially it was awarded for Boxing Championships, but from 1949 it was presented to the winner of the National First Aid Competition. Such a successful team created a great interest in first aid and resulted in the formation of junior teams and an annual Parkside Competition. It took place at the colliery in a mock tunnel and face that had been originally erected on the surface for the Safety Competition. Over the team's successful years many of its members are worthy of note: Brian Talbot, who became Assistant Director of the Midlands and Wales Group, Stan Horsfield, who became NUM Secretary and later Area NUM Agent, Alf Downes, the later team instructor, Frank Atherton, the Safety Engineer, Alan Davies, colliery deputy, Stewart Greenall, colliery electrician and Sid Hichisson, senior Overman. The team was instructed, supported and greatly assisted by Sister Fish, the colliery nursing sister. On the whole the Parkside First Aid Team brought a feeling of pride and achievement to the colliery, with the Mitchell Hedges Trophy being displayed, drunk from, photographed and sat in by various young ladies.

Parkside First Aid Team.

The Golf Society was established in the late 1970's by Les Marsh and Len Head, two of the colliery's officials. Les Marsh was the early main-stay of the society, being at one time a county player and having a long association with the sport. In the early days the Wigan rugby player, Frank Collier, was a member, much to the concern of Les. At one meeting he turned up in a pair of cricket boots, a pit glove and a cherry and white bob-hat. The society was nearly banned from that club when Frank was caught by a group of lady members relieving himself at the side of the 9th fairway. The present President, John Genner, our heavyweight lampman, has been a member of the society since its beginning. Over the years he has had to make certain adjustments to his swing, due to his increase in girth.

Parkside Colliery Amateur Rugby League Club was formed in 1981 by a group of apprentices under the tutorship of Mick Corns. They entered an NCB Sevens competition that was held annually at Leigh Miners. The team came second in the competition and it created a great deal of interest at the pit. Mick Corns was approached with a view to forming a pit team and after a meeting at Newton Labour Club he was elected as secretary and treasurer, with Frank Pojunas as Chairman. Money was acquired from the Welfare to set up the club and further money was raised by a weekly draw at the colliery. The club proved to be very successful, being promoted season after season in their climb up the divisions. Tragedy struck the team when 3 players were involved in a car crash after a game at Culcheth; Shaun Johnson was killed, Keith Scrivens and Gary Dooney were seriously injured. The team won the Premier Division that year and Shaun's No.13 jersey is kept in a case at the club.

Over the years many of the players went on to better things, playing for professional clubs in the area:-

J. Harrison, S. Lea, I. Green - St. Helens.
D. Ellison, S. Chambers, M. Neal - Leigh.
P. Sumner - Warrington.
A. Irland - Widnes.
S. Wills, W. Bloor, P. Melling, G. Melling - Blackpool.
P. O'Keefe - Rochdale.
P. Norman, M. Edwards, S. Heaton, D. Riley - Oldham.

To discover talent in the literature field we need go no further than the pit poets. One of them, Tom Berry of Haydock, looked on himself as an ordinary chap, but he had an ability to observe life and put it to verse. Here are two of his poems:-

A DAY ON L5.

It was a typical day on L5
The coal was flowing fast.
When Harry Rudd and Crossland
Came slowly whizzing past.
Up spoke a big bold chocker,
By the name of Lazy Bob,
'If tho doesn't slow t'machine down
Ah'll hit thi in thi gob'.

In came short legged Dennis,
With one of his favourite calls,
'Get that bloody rip down'.
But Joe Cain shouted 'Balls'.
And the main man in the district,
Known as 'Adolf' Greaves
Screams and shouts on t'telephone
But never rolls up his sleeves.

The Main Gate stable Deputy,
Is commonly known as God,
But his name is Kenny Walker
A great big stupid Sod.
And the hard worked Main Gate Rippers,
Hosker, Barnes and Holmes,
Sit in the road so motionless
Tho'd think they were three stone gnomes.

Now the moral of this story is
That the management want coal,
But Pricey and his hooligans
Will drive them up the pole.
For little awkward Kenny
As awkward as can be
Say's 'You can scream your bloody yeads off
but you'll get no coal from me'.

OPPORTUNITY KNOCKS.

Opportunity knocks for all those knockers,
Who blame the miners, they're off their rockers,
'Get back to Work', you've heard them say,
Why! We haven't been on strike a day.
We're not so popular, but we have our uses,
If it's only for Heath to make excuses,
And blame us for his own mis-doings,
Which are bringing Britain down to ruins,
Ted knows what brought about this crisis,
The Common Market, and rising prices,
It's robbery, to say the least,
The way the public have been fleeced,
To France, we had to bow the knee,
Then came Ted's phases, One, Two, Three,
We're all agreed, he is a snorter
At doing things he hadn't oughter,
He's a better comic than Charlie Chaplin,
When with our problems he is grapplin',
There is no doubt, Ted and his cronies,
Are nothing but a lot of Phonies,
It's time we had a big election,
We couldn't make a worse selection,
Ted's putting millions on the dole,
Before he'll bend, Lord Bless his soul.
Now! 'Who can carry back the can'?,
Why! The Miner and his o'er-time ban,
But Ted has made a big mistake,
The NUM he'll never break,
If he won't pay, then he'll regret it;
If he wants coal, well, let him get it,
From our endeavour we must not shrink,
No matter what the public think,
To those who'll work three days a week,

And new employment have to seek;
I beg you, don't look on the dark side,
They're wanting men at Bold, and Parkside,
So now's your chance to make a flit,
And find out what it's like down pit,
The coal is brittle; The roof's like plastic
And Miner's wages are fantastic,
It's on the News; It's in the Press;
(A gimmick by those who've caused this mess),
Just fancy, soon you would be wealthy,
As fit as fiddles. Hale and healthy,
This chance was surely heaven-sent,
You could then afford Ted's unfair rent,
You'd get cheap fuel, and when sixty five,
A pension (you've paid for), if still alive,
So hurry up lads, do not wait,
Join the queue, or you'll be late;
Fifty pound, plus? What could be finer?
And just imagine; You'd be a Miner.

Another of the pit-poets was Jacky Atherton, who produced the next two rib-ticklers:-

THE GRAND ONION SHOW.

This story began many years ago
After poor results at an onion show
So Sid decided to shop around
And plant his onions on foreign ground

He contacted a gardener from Shevington moor
Whose onion growing was renowned for sure
With a garden the size of a football pitch
He could grow his onions without a hitch

Can you grow giant onions Sidney cried
Just leave it to me the gardener replied
I'm renowned far and wide as an onion grower
I've even given lessons to Percy Thrower

So plans were drawn up for tilling the ground
But a suitable chargeman had to be found
He had to be clever able and willing
So they consulted an expert by the name of George Pilling

The expert arrived with the tools of his trade
A fork and a hoe and a number three spade
On testing the ground he found to his dismay
It consisted of shingle ironstone and clay

This job is too big for a pick and a spade
An urgent decision will have to be made
I suggest dets and powder and maybe a jigger
But to make doubly sure we'll hire a digger

The equipment arrived the very next day
And the work was started without any delay
Listen said Sid there's no going slow
I want to compete in the next onion show

Don't worry about the digging the gardener replied
I've experience digging pipelines from Iraq to Port Said
For drilling and firing and blasting technique
You'll find no one better if you searched for a week

That's pure fabrication the expert replied
You've done all your work at Robin Hill and Parkside
As for drilling and firing and blasting technique
I've had no experience and therefore can't speak

To save further argument Sidney stepped in
You can both grow my onions he said with a grin
So let's get cracking and prepare the ground
For the onion season will soon be around

So work went ahead with amazing speed
And Sidney sent off for his onion seed
Lorry loads of top soil arrived in bulk
But the expert stood back and started to sulk

Come now said Sidney let's work as a team
I'm trying to fulfil a lifetimes dream
If these giant onions turn out a success
I'll guarantee you both 12 months S and S

As long as the're dayshifts the expert replied
I'll throw in my lot count me on your side
Hold on said the gardener I don't work weekends
But regular day outbye will soon make amends

They phoned all the farmers for miles around
Send all your shit to put on our ground
We'll spread it in layers 10 inches thick
And leave it for Sid to stir with his stick

The onions grew to a colossal size
With these gloated Sidney I'll take the first prize
We'll lift them tomorrow on the eve of the show
With the aid of an air hoist turfor and hoe

The onions were lifted and loaded to go
By road, rail and canal to the grand Blackpool show
They kept guard in watches and when they changed over
Gazed in pride at three onions on a low loader

They arrived in Blackpool the following noon
To be put on display in the tower ballroom
The police flashed a message they'll be here in an hour
And an air hoist was hurriedly fixed up to the tower

With air hoist set up and roof section removed
They were lowered into the ballroom there to be viewed
Sidney walked in to a standing ovation
Led by the chairman of the onion growers' federation

Well done said the Mayor as he shook Sidney's hand
I've never seen onions so big and so grand
Mine aren't as good not one little bit
Tell me your secret do you use special shit

Just hard work said Sidney hard work alone
I've grown these three onions all on my own
Up on the balcony overlooking the stage
The expert and gardener were trembling with rage

The judges walked in to a clapping of hands
And a fanfare of trumpets from Black Dyke Mills Band
They stared in amazement their mouths open wide
While Sidney looked on his chest swollen with pride

Sidney winning first prize was a foregone conclusion
But winning all three would smell of collusion
The panel of judges was split down the middle
To award all three prizes would look like a fiddle

The judges arguments were long and loud
So an arbitrator was called for out of the crowd
Sidney's heart leaped and down dropped his jaw
When out of the crowd walked Overman Shaw

Shaw was invited to hand out the passes
But unfortunately Derek had mislaid his glasses
Sorry he muttered I haven't a clue
Give him ten out of ten I'll leave it to you

With the arbitrator's casting vote
Sidney smiled and began to gloat
The prizes at last he chuckled are mine
But the gardener shouted hold on take your time

Backed by the expert he jumped onto the stand
And pointed at Sid with a trembling hand
For growing these onions you've taken the credit for sure
But these onions were grown at Shevington Moor

Overman Shaw burst onto the scene
That's the meanest trick I've ever seen
I appeal to the judges that these entries be scratched
Because they were grown on an illegal patch

Sid crawled out of the Ballroom in utter disgrace
And a smile appeared on the gardeners face
But the expert was horrified and began to protest
Do you realise I've just lost 12 months S and S

THE GANGSTER.

Here is a story with nothing to hide
Of a security problem that arose at Parkside
The pickets had gathered, tension in the air
The security chief wrung his hands in despair
I can't stand it he cried, his voice broke with a sob
I need a good man for controlling this mob

He approached personnel and asked for advice
They told him the rules are you must advertise
Bugger the rules, we swim or we sink
We'll soon get around that, replied Chris with a wink
Listen he said with a frown on his face
I have such a man, but he's still in disgrace

Ron Silver spoke up, his head in his hands
I'm desperate he muttered, tell me your plans
Chris replied with a wink and a nod
I might just have the right man for the job
We all know of course he won't have a beano
He's and ex-enforcer from Wigan Casino

Not him cried Silver we're already on the rocks
If he gets the job, it's goodbye to the stocks
But as they were desperate and at their wits' end
They decided for once the rules they could bend
Right muttered Silver, he'd better be good
He picked up the phone and rang Harry Rudd

Harry he said we're in a right hole
We're having a problem with picket control
It's been suggested to Chris and myself
There's a member of NACODS can handle himself
We prefer a man with his deputy's ticket
Someone quite fearless when facing the picket

Right said Harry, I might have an answer
We have just the fellow, we call him the gangster
He's a real rough handful, he knows every trick
In the RAF police they called him Mad Mick
But be very careful, if that's your intention
He's still under threat of a fine and suspension

They rang 103 and the message was blunt
You're wanted immediately in the top shunt
Drop what your doing, come right away
Gangster was shaking his head in dismay
I know he cried, it's happened at last
Someone's unearthed my unsavoury past

A loco was waiting and whisked him outbye
Straight up the pit, in the blink of an eye
He slowly entered the packed conference room
Hanging his head his face full of gloom
But the management gave him a standing ovation
For he held a diploma from the strike breakers federation

'The very Man' cried the security chief
As he gazed in admiration at gangster's physique
Men of your calibre are thin on the ground
But are you sure you're not muscle bound
Gangster just laughed and rocked back on his heels
Then flexed his muscles to the tune of wheels

We're having picket problems the manager cried
Just leave it with me sir the gangster replied
I've handled mass pickets before now he grinned
Apart from their leader, the're all piss and wind
Get him cried the manager, I'm telling you all
I want the Yorkshire bastard nailed to the wall

Just a minute said the gangster as they voiced their accord
If I break up the picket line what's my reward
The area manager rose to the bait
We'll forget the past you'll have a clean slate
And to show the management's not entirely bent
All the coal you can carry without harassment

Word reached the picket line later that day
A professional strike-breaker was on his way
Let him come cried their leader, a man among men
A hulking six footer called Slavering Ben
Noted for violence, a hard man to please
A sadistic ex-corporal of the military police

Who is this strike-breaker the picket leader cried
It's Mad Mick the gangster someone replied
He felt his heartbeat beginning to race
He emptied his bowels, the blood drained from his face
Not gangster he whispered, his voice hoarse with fear
Just then came the sound of the management cheer

Listen lads said Ben you all heard that cheer
Any minute now gangsters bound to appear
He once quelled a riot, and appeared on the telly
He has four double chins and a beer bloated belly
But don't let that fool you. In one of his raids
He broke up a picket line with Ajax's grenades

When gangster appeared they stopped in their tracks
He was pushing a mine-car with some well filled sacks
Ben went to meet him and started to squirm

He asked for surrender with honourable terms
No way said the gangster by now sorely vexed
I'm going to bombard you with Coventry Rejects

Let battle commence then by foul means or fair
I'll break up this picket line with three bags to spare
But the pickets were scattering away from the mine
They ran for their cars on the A49
Back to Barnsley cried Ben and make it quick
Even Scargill himself won't face up to Mad Mick

Well done cried the manager your missions completed
The pickets are scattered, their leader defeated
I can only say we're all very proud
And now it's back to your work underground
But to make doubly sure your coal's out of sight
Come on next week from six to midnight

In glamour Parkside has been blessed with some very special beauties. Over a purple patch of 5 years, from 1978 to 1984, most of the Parkside Coal Queens were highly placed in the National Coal Queen finals. The first of them was Ann Melling, the daughter of Alan Melling, the colliery deputy. In 1978 Ann Melling won the Miss Parkside title, then the Lancashire title, followed by the National title. Two years later Yvonne McCann took the same route, becoming runner-up in the National finals. However, she took over the mantle of National Coal Queen and carried out all the duties, because the initial winner relinquished the crown. The next glamour girl, in 1982, was Carol Hilton, the daughter of Frank Hilton. a face worker. Carol Hilton was runner-up in the National finals and over the years has held many beauty titles. A year later Cheryl Goulding, the daughter of Ken Goulding, became Miss Parkside. She then won the Lancashire title and came third in the National finals.

The Safety Quiz Teams began at Parkside in 1978, with the formation of a junior and a senior team. Safety Quizzes had been introduced into the coal industry to promote, encourage and expand knowledge in safety matters. The Parkside Junior team won the very first Area Competition and were to dominate it for the next six years. In 1982 they won the National Safety Quiz Final, when the members were Andrew Shakeshaft, Derek Hill, Chris Speed, David Davies and reserve Paul Prescott. In 1979 Dave Unsworth, the Junior Team captain won the sub-area section of the newly formed Safety Mind Individual Competition. He then won the Area final and represented the Western Area in the National Finals, becoming runner-up. Further success came to the Parkside team when, in 1988 and 1989, they won the Target Safety Competition Group Final, earning a well deserved place in the National Finals.

Parkside Coal Queens

Above: Ann Melling underground at Parkside.

Right: Carol Hilton and her father Frank.

Parkside Coal Queens

Above: Cheryl Goulding with Kevin Singleton, Mark Hutchinson and Harry Hutchinson.

Right: Yvonne McCann.

The Chess Club formed in the 1970's, when Golborne Chess Club changed their name and venue to Parkside. They have had some success in the Warrington Chess League and at one time entertained an International Master at the colliery. Ken Horne, the assistant manager, has been involved with the club throughout most of its existence. He is well known for his adjourned games, which sometimes went on for weeks. During one of those games he became so mentally involved in the moves that he drove past the colliery and ended up in Warrington, instead of coming to work.

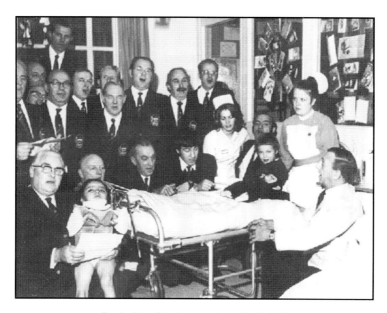

Parkside Choir on a hospital visit.

Parkside Colliery has become famous throughout the country due to the singing ability of its Male Voice Choir. John Watkins, one of its mainstays, has been a member for many years and can relate some of its history:-

"The formation of the choir took place in February 1970, through an idea by one of its Mechanical Engineers, Mr. Horace Smith. From modest beginnings it has grown in stature to become one of the most successful and sought after choirs in the North West. The Choir has performed regularly throughout the area and has given in excess of 400 performances for charitable causes. They have taken part in Massed Choir Concerts at Preston, Liverpool and Manchester, also appearing on TV programmes such as 'Stars on Sunday' and 'A Grand Sing', as well as local radio. Probably the most memorable performances were given in the Royal Albert Hall for the 31st Burma Star Reunion with Dame Vera Lynn, and leading the morning service in St. George's Chapel, Windsor. Our first

tape recording, 'Stout Hearted Men', was made in October 1989 and has proved so successful that a second tape, 'Comrades', was made in September 1990. The 60+ voices represent a wide range of occupations and professions, not only from the mining industry but also teachers, engineers, administrators and retired gentlemen, who travel from the areas of Wigan, St. Helens, Newton, Leigh, Ashton, Standish and Tyldesley.

The 'pit story' of how the choir began, is that one day Horace Smith and Jimmy Scarborough, two mechanical engineers, were deeply involved in a breakdown on the Coal Prep Plant. Having reached the stage that sometimes happens during colliery breakdowns, when nothing is going right and then comes the dreaded phone call from the manager saying, 'when is it going to run again?,' or words to that effect. One of them is supposed to have said to the other, 'well, what are we going to do now?,' the reply was, 'Let's have a sing-song!' From that small idea, Horace Smith produced the Parkside Choir.

In the future Parkside Male Voice Choir will be the only link with the past, and it is hoped that they will retain their colliery name.

CHARACTERS AND WORKERS.

Parkside Colliery, like many other pits, had its quota of characters. These were people that possessed a certain outlook or turn of phrase that caused amusement to the rest of the work-force. Their attitude to life was different from that of the ordinary man and set them apart. Pit stories about these characters would begin with some grain of truth and then be exaggerated, twisted and changed to be completely different. The attributes and aspects of the men that took part would be blown out of all proportions, with some becoming gods and demons alike.

Over the years many characters have worked at the pit and it is impossible to mention them all. The first characters that were met at the colliery were the Lampmen. Their main job was giving out and maintaining the pit lamps. Some of their names spring to mind: Bill Hornby, an upright personality of great authority, Tommy Leyland, a friendly semi-retired fireman, big gruff Tommy Birk, Michael Houghton, who was known as 'Metal Mickey' because of his injured leg and John Genner, the semi-retired electrician. John was an aggressive, bouncy character who always remarked that he did not eat or drink much, but was still over 20 stone in weight. He could eat his own 'snap', anybody else's and still send out for fish and chips.

On the pit-bank there were characters such as Billy Ablitt, the Banksman. He was a man full of life and vigour who controlled the pit-bank on three shifts, besides having two or three other jobs as well. Billy was actually born in Bryn, near Ashton, but was raised in Kent. Everybody knew

Ken Hiley.

when he visited his favourite town, Ramsgate, because he suddenly acquired a southern twang. Most of his actions were illegal and would not have been tolerated in the present day, a sad loss in a boring world. Billy was not a man to cross, especially if you were still in the cage. Any trouble maker was either left in the cold at ground level, sent back down the pit, or washed down with the fire hose. Billy's favourite terms were: 'tea and cakes, girls', 'who's a big boy then?' and, to the pit men, 'Now Dears, are you going down today?' Other Banksmen deserve a mention: Les Jones, nowty Wilf Houghton, the ex-army man Bill Woollard, Jimmy Charnock, grumpy Pee Newall, Jed Myler and John Carney, who was known as the smallest banksman in the north-west.

The ride down the pit at Parkside was quite a gentle one, when compared to the old steam winders. The cages were controlled by the Winding Engine-men or Winders as they were termed. The job always had a great tradition attached to it. In the past it was either passed down from father to son or men were promoted from other related jobs like Boilerman or Banksman. They were normally regular workers in their fifties, who had little home life because of the hours they worked, but at the end of the pit's life younger men were drafted in. Some of the older men were masters of their craft: George Shaw, Arthur Whitter, Bert Baines, Danny Jones and Benny Walls were all worthy of note. Other Winders had certain characteristics: Bob Selby, the marathon running fitness freak, Bill Marrow, the moustached executive, Len Hart, or 'old tupper' as he was called, Keith Horsfield, the radio ham and many others.

At the pit bottom the Onsetters were in charge of the loading and unloading of the cages. Over the years many men have done the job: the brothers Calderbank, Tommy Wilcox, known as 'Phyllis', Ken Pennington, or KP as he was known, Kenny Hiley, the hunting, shooting and fishing extrovert. Kenny had lost some of his fingers in a shooting accident, but this did not stop him working afternoons and nights, as long as the char were not biting. Most of the others have faded into the history of the pit but some can be remembered: Harold Clarke, the nose-twisting, leg-grabber from Wigan, who was a man not to be laughed at, Harold Haydock, Benny Walls, Tommy

Hesketh, the crossword expert and Jimmy Pollock, all played their part in the running of the pit.

In the late sixties the sanitary conditions at the pit were appalling, with it not being safe to venture near the manholes set aside for that purpose. Our saving grace was Tommy Cherry. He had come from one of the Wigan pits to Parkside and was immediately put in charge of "The Bins". Within a few weeks things had completely changed. Manholes were painted, American-style saloon doors were fitted, bins were changed weekly and the greatest luxury of all appeared, toilet paper. He had some funny little traits, like eating while he cleaned out the toilets and offering everybody that passed him a boiled sweet. It was said that he kept a bag of sweets all week due to the lack of takers.

Another great character from the early days was Bill Potter, who took charge of the new apprentices. He was a Wiganer with a hilarious turn of phrase totally incomprehensible to an outsider. Such terms as 'I'll give you a comic singer's lip' and 'I'll make your mouth so as it won't hold warm tea' have little meaning today. Others like 'tighten her green lines' and 'grease her bottom pulleys', with their sexual connotation, wouldn't be understood outside pit life. Bill was certainly the finest deliverer of the one-line put down in the history of the pit. One of his best was the remark about the chief time clerk, who was referred to as 'the fastest man alive over 3 yards'. The chief time clerk was one of the most misunderstood and disliked men at a pit, and the three yards was the distance from the time office window to the door to lock it, to stop anybody thumping him.

One of our more flamboyant characters was Terry Crook, the deputy, who was always known as Doggy. He was an aggressive and pugnacious character and when he was around there was never a peaceful moment. His nickname had been with him throughout all of his career as an official. It began innocently enough when he was doing his Deputy's training at Astley Green Colliery:-

"During my training I had to follow the Supervising Deputy, Harry Gaynor, everywhere during his shift. One day on the face the cutter man, Frank Butler, remarked, 'Hey up here's Harry with his little dog'. I've had that nickname for the last 25 years."

At Parkside his name was sometimes used in a derogatory sense, with many tricks being played on him by his fellow officials and the men. However this usually resulted in someone being threatened by a very large fist!

The above fist was sometimes used on one of our most famous and infamous characters at the pit, Sid Hichisson, although not without some threat applied in return. Little Sid, as he was known, was one of the most feared officials at the pit. He always required total commitment to the job and, knowing the laziness of some of the miners, he did not go down too well

Frank Groves, Sid Hichisson and Norman Harrison.

in some quarters. Sid was born in Clapham, London and only came to this part of the country because of the Blitz. After training at Low Hall and Wigan Junction Colliery Sid worked at John Pit and Bickershaw Colliery, before moving to Parkside in 1964. By that time he had reached the level of Overman and was deeply involved in first aid training and competitions. During his time at Parkside he became John Connaughton's right hand man in the never-ending and fruitless task of trying to keep the men at their work. Sid was known for his strictness and discipline at the pit and many jokes, poems and graffiti were written about him. His favourite motto was that you're not a good boss if your name does not appear on a toilet door - his name appeared all over the pit.

One John Connaughton - Sid Hichisson story went as follows:-

John: 'Sid, we've got to stop these men getting on the rider early.'
Sid: 'Yes John.'
John: 'I want you to station an official at the bottom of the rider, to control them.'
Sid: 'Right John.'
Next day.
John: 'Sid, did you put an official at the bottom of the rider?'
Sid: 'Yes John.'
John: 'Who was it?'
Sid: 'Dickey Pilk.'
John, voice rising: 'Dickey Pilk! Dickey Pilk! But who's going to control Dickey Pilk?'

Dickey Pilkington and his mate, Jackie Platt, were two of the biggest joke players and wisecrackers at the pit.

Many other officials can be recalled: Jimmy Holmes, Jack Mawdesley, Bill Rooney, Jimmy Shacklady, Frank Garvin, Jimmy Norris, Wally Thomas, Roy Gwyllam, Brian Carey, Matt Smith, Sid Lawrenson, Ronny Pye, Harold Crosland, Gerald Eaves and more recently Ray Hall, Pee Wolf and Norman Shaw, the list can carry on for ever. At one time in the seventies all senior officials wanted to be called MISTER, in capitals. One of the night-turn undermanagers developed the disease and told one of the men to call him Mister Pye in future. The reply was, 'I'll call you prater pie but never Mr. Pye',- another pit tale!

Three men not on the above list must be mentioned individually: Jack Ellis, Frankie Collier and Derek Shaw. Jack Ellis, was a Bevin Boy from Dorset. He worked at other local pits and was then drafted to Parkside in 1964. Jack was always known for his strength and an attitude of 'get out of the way, I'll do it.' The pit-men would sometimes joke about this remarking, 'get out of the way, I'll be Jack Ellis today.'

Frankie Collier, was, in the sixties, famous throughout the country, as well as at the pit. Besides holding down a job at the pit , Frank was a second row forward for Wigan Rugby League Club. He was a massive individual not known for his subtleties and was awarded the Lance Todd Trophy at Wembley for best player.

Lastly, Derek Shaw, was a fiery and bombastic character who was well known for his comical stories and sayings. One of his most famous encounters was with Mr. Vincent, the Mines Inspector:-

Mr. Vincent: 'I could have done with you coming around L30's with me.'
Derek Shaw: 'Oh no Mr. Vincent, I've got a little dog at home and he only understands four words, one is food and when he hears that he sits up and begs, another is walkies and when he hears that he stands at the door with his tail wagging, the other words are Mr. Vincent, and when he hears that he shoots under the table because he knows he's going to get a kick up the backside.'

Inbye at the colliery an endless list of characters would be encountered, with their comical remarks and actions. Ronnie Sankey, Derek Johnson and Bob Scrivens were the Belt-men and Jackie Three Brow was one of the Button-men who got his nickname by the way he answered the phone. Fitters and Electricians could be normally found settled in their own cabins, awaiting a breakdown, some contemplating the inside of their eye-lids. Others like Jimmy Wood, Frank Groves, Phil Bond, Pee Harrison, Kenny Thompson, Graham Burke, Frank Stone, John Johnson, Stan Morris, Jack Critchley, Merv the swerve, Billy Lathom, known as Billy Whiz were well known tradesmen. Frankie Groves was a pocket powerhouse from Wigan, who was always known for carrying large pieces of machinery.

Frank was also known for spending more time at the pit than the canteen cat. One pit story was that his wife finally persuaded him to go on a fortnight's holiday. During the two weeks a banging noise was heard in the baths and when it was tracked down they found it was Frankie's boots trying to get out and go underground. Major officials, like Overmen, Undermanagers and Managers, usually came underground later than everybody else and a secret signalling system came in operation when they appeared. Flashing lights, coded signals, DAC messages all warned the unwary of the impending visit.

Jack Meadows receiving his welfare prize from Peter Dooley.
Also in the group are Bob Jacques and Bill Shaw.

Face-men were another group of workers that warranted respect. They worked at the cutting edge of coal production and some of them were very tough characters, being used to hard and dirty toil. Chock men, Cutter men, Stable-end men, Rippers and 'Bummers' are names connected with coal face work. Men such as: Bob Jacques, Don Gerrard, Joe Carney, Stan Speakman, Sammy Podmore, Kenny Westhead, Joe Holden, Jimmy McLoughlin, Bill Ashton, Jacky Meadows, Dicky Cross are just a few of many that could be named. Adam Kuzio, a Cutterman of repute, still remembers his days at the pit:-

"I was born in the Ukraine, but was classed as a displaced person in Europe after the 2nd World War. They promised us any job that we wanted if we came to Britain, but when we got here there was only the pits and farming. I worked at 8 collieries before Parkside and I've always thought that it was the best pit. I'll always remember when Lord Robens came round L40s, he said to us, 'Don't call me Sir just call me Alf.' In those

days there were about 30 men to every face, which changed drastically towards the end."

Frank King, face Charge-hand and later union representative, reflects on his work and work-mates at the pit:-

"Face work was hard but rewarding and I think if I had the chance I'd go back down pit tomorrow. For the majority of the time we worked well with management and I've always looked on the Coal Board as a good employer. George Catteral was the greatest character that I ever met. He'd been everywhere in the world and seen it, done it, and caught it. George was one of the best storytellers and used to say, 'I can get more round me than the Pope' and was very critical of modern managers, 'Managers shouldn't wear cuff links they should have blue scars.' I was proud to be associated with the men I met at Parkside and thank them for their support through the years in union and work matters."

Fred Hazelden.

Surface workers were a different breed to the underground men. Pit-men thought they contributed little to the running of the pit, but all workers should be given some credit in the production of coal. The workshops were full of long-term workers, or in-mates, in a type of clique that could never be split. Initially they were workers from other pits, then a group of young men grew into, and established themselves in the job. The Fitting Shop began with men like Joe Lindsey, Jack Carter, Frank Jackson, Roy Davis (Nobum), Derek Smith and Peter Daniels. At the end of the pit's life other men had taken over: Sandy Atherton, otherwise known as Supertap, Freddy (the Rat) Hazelden, Mick Morrisey, Jimmy Dawber, Geoff (Spud) Seddon, Teddy (Handbag) Perry and Norman Pilling, who always remarked, 'Hast eard owt?' The workshop men were never completely controlled by management, sometimes making their own rules. They teamed up on most big jobs with Blacksmiths, Welders, Joiners and Shaftsmen, such as George Simm, George Yates, who wanted to work until he was seventy, Ossie Kearney, the inventor, Ronnie Kenyon, Keith Rudd, Peter Prescott, Ronnie Bate, Jimmy Parkinson, Tommy Ince, Freddy Gee, Billy Hall, Derek Callinan, who was the Spot the Ball expert, Steve Simm, Peter Hartley, Frank Caton and, at the end, conscientious Cliff Graham. The type of work that they carried out in the shafts was one of the most dangerous at the pit, because they were sometimes suspended over a 800 yard drop!

Workshop Electricians.
Left to right: Peter Harrison, Roy Fairhurst, Ken Green,
Jack Woodcock, Don Smith and Billy Kelly.

The electrical shop always looked on themselves as slightly superior to the rest, especially on the intelligence front. Some of them became quite famous, or infamous, in the history of the pit. Wilf Lowe, Jimmy Case, Geoff Martlew, 'Viking' Eddy Ball, Jack Woodcock, Dave O'Neill, Pee Owen, Ken Sidlow, Tony Woodacre, Colin Halliwell, Ken (Fingers) Green, 'Doctor' Roy Fairhurst and John Horrocks. John was one of the most conscientious workers at the pit, being prepared to come to work at any time of night or day. When it was known that the pit was to finish in 1993, one of the fitters jokingly scrawled on the workshop board: 'Parkside colliery closed October 1993, John Horrocks still at No.3 Horizon October 1994.'

Other surface workers including Bathsmen, Boilermen, Yardmen, Methanemen and Coal Prep. workers also played their part at the colliery. The Coal Preparation Plant, or Washery, was a different world altogether, complete with its own Manager. The Washery was one of the wettest and muckiest places at the pit, even when compared with the underground. Ronnie Baldwin, a larger than life ex-merchant seaman, spent the majority of his time at the pit on night-turn on the Washery. He was known for his story-telling, with his arms waving, eyes flashing, beard bristling, Ronnie would relate his hilarious if exaggerated tale.

Thousands of men have worked at Parkside Colliery in its short life, men from many different towns and backgrounds. Many of them worked there for most of their careers and others just for a short while. It is not possible to mention them all and I apologise to those that I have missed out. I dedicate this book to all of them, especially those that were killed and injured at the colliery, and to the British miner in general. You were unique in the working class of this country and governments will rue your passing.

"Happier Days"

Union and Management in the Conference Room - Lord Roben's visit in 1970.

Group consists of:
Alf Downes, Bert Farimond, Alan Jones, Don Gerard, Bill Corcoran, Terry O'Neil,
Frank Pelly, Bob Smith, Ronnie Wilkins, John Killmartin, Bill Ormshaw,
Lord Robens, Bill Peet, Sammy Podmore, John Gibbons, Tom Pennington,
Matt Smith, Peter Tootle, Ken Walker, Jim Shacklady, Stan Horsfield, Mick Noonan,
Bill Shaw, Wally Hope, Bill Smith, John Connaughton, Frank Atherton,
Harold Crossland, Paul Housely, Bill Holdsworth, Jack Foy, Ken Cunliffe,
Joe Finney, Frank Reid, Bob Jacques, Bill Bullen, Bill Ince and Gerald Eaves.

APPENDIX

General facts about Parkside Colliery

Area of Take .... Approximately 8 square miles
Area of Colliery site .... Approximately 76 acres
Workable Reserves .... Over 100,000,000 tonnes
Dip of Seams .... 1 in 5 south-east

Shafts

Two shafts 24ft. diameter, concrete lined, 12 in. minimum thickness

No. 1 Horizon at 449 yds. deep
No. 2 Horizon at 566 yds. deep
No. 3 Horizon at 719 yds. deep
No. 4 Horizon at 836 yds. deep
Shaft Bottom at 885 yds. deep

Winding

No. 1 Tower .... 191 ft. 6 in. high
No. 2 Tower .... 204 ft. 9 in. high
Two Winders per shaft ...... 2500 h.p.
Four ropes .... locked coil type
No. 1 Shaft .... Four deck cages and counterweights
No. 2 Shaft .... 15 ton skips and counterweights

Tunnels

Driven before production .. 19.5 Km (12.2 miles)
Driven in life of pit .... 163.3 Km (102.2 miles)
Roadway Junctions 493

Faces

Total of 76 coal faces
1 in London Delph
14 in Crombouke
13 in Ince Six Feet
33 in Lower Florida
1 in Wigan Five Feet
12 in Wigan Four Feet
2 in Trencherbone

Face	Start Date	Finish Date	Face	Start Date	Finish Date
B1	April 1964	April 1968	L44	Nov. 1976	June 1979
C1	June 1964	Sept. 1964	L43	Mar. 1977	Oct. 1978
F1	Sept. 1964	Dec. 1964	W25	May 1977	May 1978
E2	Jan. 1965	Sept.1965	W3	Nov. 1977	May 1978
F6	May 1965	Jan. 1968	S15	Feb. 1978	Mar. 1980
A2	May 1965	June 1967	L19	May 1978	Jan. 1984
D1	Dec. 1965	Mar. 1967	S100 (1)	June 1978	Sept. 1979
E3	May 1966	Sept. 1968	T24	Nov. 1978	June 1980
A1	Feb. 1967	Aug. 1967	L46	Feb. 1979	Oct. 1980
F2	Mar. 1967	Nov. 1968	L17	Mar. 1979	Dec. 1980
C2	May 1967	May 1969	W4	June 1979	June 1981
L2	Aug. 1967	July 1968	S100 (2)	Mar. 1980	Feb. 1982
L3	July 1968	May 1969	L45	June 1980	June 1981
L10	Aug. 1968	Jan. 1969	T25	Aug. 1980	June 1981
B2	Jan. 1969	June 1971	S16	Sept. 1980	April 1983
C22	Feb. 1969	Sept. 1970	L30	Feb. 1981	Nov. 1985
L11	Mar. 1969	June 1971	L48	Mar. 1981	Aug. 1981
L4	Sept. 1969 & June 1971	Sept. 1973	W5	Aug. 1981	July 1983
L21	Jan. 1970	Sept. 1970	S200	June 1982	Aug. 1983
C24	May 1970	June 1971	LD10	July 1983	Aug. 1983
L22	July 1970	Feb. 1971	W6	July 1983	Sept. 1985
C23	Aug. 1970	June 1971	L31	Sept. 1983	Oct. 1985
L40 (1)	Nov. 1970	July 1971	C15	Oct. 1983	Feb. 1986
L12	Mar. 1971	June 1973	L32	May 1985	Nov. 1986
L24	May 1971	Feb. 1973	W8	Oct. 1985	Sept. 1986
L41	Aug. 1971	Feb. 1973	V24	Oct. 1985	April 1986
L15	Mar. 1972	July 1974	L33	Mar. 1986	July 1987
L23	Dec. 1972	May 1974	C16	Sept. 1986	May 1987
L5	Mar. 1973	May 1975	W11	Oct. 1986	Jan. 1988
L40 (2)	Mar. 1973	May 1975	S31	July 1987	Sept. 1989
S10	Aug. 1973	Nov. 1975	W15	Dec. 1987	Jan. 1989
L18	Dec. 1973	May 1978	S32	Dec. 1988	Oct. 1990
L42	April 1974	May 1974	W17	April 1989	Jan. 1990
L14	May 1974	Aug. 1975	W32	Jan. 1990	Sept. 1991
L16	Nov. 1974	Dec. 1976	S33	Mar. 1990	July 1991
S4	June 1975	April 1977	S34	July 1991	Oct. 1992
W24	Aug. 1975	May 1977	W31	Aug. 1991	Oct. 1992
S11	Mar. 1976	July 1977	S35	Oct. 1992	Oct. 1992

SALEABLE TONS

YEAR	TONS	TONNES	O.M.S. (Cwts)	O.M.S. (Tons)	O.M.S. (Tonnes)	MEN ON BOOKS
1958						12
1959						47
1960						101
1961						184
1962	2019	2051				286
1963/4	22747	23110				451
1964/5	243270	247162	28.70	1.45	1.47	987
1965/6	353828	359489	30.20	1.51	1.53	1192
1966/7	433329	440262	29.60	1.48	1.50	1377
1967/8	580000	589280	35.50	1.77	1.80	1534
1968/9	636475	646658	38.70	1.94	1.97	1550
1969/70	650097	660498	37.70	1.89	1.92	1573
1970/1	589845	599282	33.30	1.66	1.69	1648
*1971/2	488857	496678	29.58	1.48	1.50	1753
1972/3	739000	750824	39.50	1.98	2.01	1738
*1973/4	516978	525249	33.30	1.66	1.69	1683
1974/5	693318	704411	39.50	1.98	2.01	1662
1975/6	761672	773858	44.40	2.22	2.25	1653
1976/7	599173	608759	35.60	1.78	1.81	1652
1977/8	611769	621557	36.50	1.83	1.86	1686
1978/9	810174	823137	40.06	2.00	2.03	1718
1979/80	831566	844871	47.04	2.35	2.39	1728
1980/1	790766	803419	45.08	2.25	2.29	1743
1981/2	840378	853824	48.62	2.43	2.47	1712
1982/3	836986	850378	47.44	2.37	2.41	1732
*1983/4	545016	553736	34.25	1.71	1.74	1675
*1984/5	261681	265868	29.33	1.47	1.49	1653
1985/6	742895	754781	45.28	2.26	2.30	1631
1986/7	813049	826058	55.51	2.78	2.82	1335
1987/8	846470	860014	71.26	3.56	3.62	1045
1988/9	822373	835531	70.67	3.53	3.59	978
1989/90	856072	869769	80.91	4.05	4.11	868
1990/1	966288	981749	97.24	4.86	4.94	803
1991/2	856816	870525	93.50	4.68	4.75	756
1992/3	413663	420282	68.50	3.43	3.48	661

*   Results affected by national disputes

Total saleable since 1962:-   19,156570   Tons

Total saleable since 1962:-   19,463075   Tonnes